齊物
逍遙

2 0 1 8

黃效文───

著

ENLIGHTENED SOJOURN

Authored and Photographed by Wong How Man

Wong How Man

Time Magazine honored Wong How Man among their 25 Asian Heroes, calling Wong "China's most accomplished living explorer". The same honor was bestowed on Aung San Suu Kyi, the Karmapa, Yao Ming and Jackie Chan, among others. CNN has featured his work over a dozen times, including a half-hour profile by anchor Richard Quest. Discovery Channel has made several documentaries about his work.

Wong began exploring China in 1974. He is Founder/President of the China Exploration & Research Society, a non-profit organization specializing in exploration, research, conservation and education in remote China and neighboring countries. Wong has led six major expeditions for the National Geographic. He successfully defined the sources of the Yangtze, Mekong, Yellow River, Salween, Irrawaddy and the Brahmaputra rivers.

His organization conducts conservation projects covering China and neighboring countries, including Nepal, Laos, Bhutan, the Philippines, and Myanmar. Wong has authored over twenty books. Wong has received an honorary doctorate from his alma mater, the University of Wisconsin, and the Lifetime Achievement Award from Monk Hsing Yun of Taiwan.

黃
效
文

《時代雜誌》曾選黃效文為亞洲二十五位英雄之一，稱他為「中國最有成就的在世探險家」。這樣的殊榮曾頒發給翁山蘇姬，噶瑪巴，姚明，成龍，還有其他在各領域傑出的人士。CNN 報導過黃效文所做的事超過十二次之多，其中還包括主播 Richard Quest 的三十分鐘專訪。探索頻道也為他做的工作製作了好幾個紀錄片。

黃效文自一九七四年開始在中國探險。他是中國探險學會的創辦人也是會長，這是個非營利組織，致力於在中國偏遠地區跟鄰近國家的探險，研究，保育跟教育工作。他成功地定位長江，湄公河，黃河，薩爾溫江，伊洛瓦底江及雅魯藏布江的源頭。

他的學會主導的保育項目橫跨中國和鄰近的國家，包括尼泊爾，寮國，不丹，菲律賓與緬甸。黃效文出版的書超過二十本。他的母校威斯康辛大學頒發給他名譽博士學位，星雲大師也贈與他「華人世界終身成就獎」。

Foreword

by F Sionil José

September 15, 2018

It is not every week that How Man Wong visits Manila, but ever since meeting him for the first time some years ago, I have always looked forward to seeing him again.

How Man always brings new insights to so many of the problems that trouble us in the region today. More than this, with his vast knowledge of the region and elsewhere -- both the cosmopolitan and the distant, neglected, ravaged, or undiscovered parts of the world -- he is able to bring a sense of order to so many of the complex and chaotic issues that bedevil us.

What How Man does is not really reduce complicated subjects to their simplest level. Take for instance the first book of his that I read, Islamic Frontiers of China. What impressed me the most is the variety of cultures in that vast country and, therefore, the great challenges that its leaders have to surmount in their efforts to unify, govern, and develop the continent. It is for this reason that I have always admired China's leaders -- Mao Zedong, Deng Xiaoping, Zhou Enlai -- for unifying China and for providing it with a bureaucracy and entrepreneurship that have taken China from poverty to become the richest country in the world today.

On a very personal level, I have found with How Man many mutual interests -- the vast variety of Chinese cooking, for instance, which I never really appreciated until my family lived in Hong Kong for a couple of years in the early 1960s. We talked about the complexity of Chinese cuisine and our delight in learning about very simple or exotic dishes.

Then, too, he is fond of motorcycles, of Harleys, with which I have always been in love since I was a teenager. And pipes -- I have always looked with awe at men who smoke pipes -- they are real characters. There was a time I wanted a Meerschaum for myself, except I gave up smoking a long time ago and would not resume it. But still I would imagine a Meerschaum pipe looking marvelous on my desk.

How Man has travelled all over the world, and has written easy-to-read reports about the places he has seen, the people he has met, giving them all an immediate charm. He also has many humanitarian interests in Southeast Asia. In several islands of Palawan in the Philippines, he defines his work as finding paths to self-sufficiency, modernization and progress that allow communities to benefit from their resource-rich lands and seas because they are also nurturing and protecting them.

How Man's interest in the cultures of other people goes beyond human curiosity; it is a search as well for the values that underpin these societies. And as he describes their lives, we find in them commonalities and, in the process, discover our own humanity. We are all equal.

推薦序

弗朗西斯科·西奧尼爾·何塞

黃效文難得才會來到馬尼拉，但幾年前和他第一次碰面後，就一直期待能再和他相聚敘舊。

因為效文不僅對這個地區，還包括了其他的地方，像是都會、偏鄉、弱勢、飽受摧殘或世所未知的地方，都有非常深入的了解，因此總能為我們所面臨的諸多問題帶來新的洞見，甚至能夠幫助我們釐清這些困擾的難題。

效文並不完全只是將複雜的問題簡單化，例如我讀過他的一本書《中國伊斯蘭文化的邊疆》（*Islamic Frontiers of China*），其中最讓我印象深刻的，是中國這樣大的國家擁有如此多元的文化，也因此政府在凝聚民心、治理國家和發展經濟的過程中，必須克服艱鉅的挑戰，這也是我非常佩服像毛澤東、鄧小平或周恩來這些中國領袖的原因，他們凝聚全民，藉著建立官僚體系和創業精神，讓中國擺脫窮困成為現今全世界最富裕的國家之一。

以個人的角度來看，我和效文有頗多共同的興趣，像是中國料理，一九六零年代初我們舉家搬到香港住了幾年後，我才真正懂得欣賞中國料理的多樣性。我們聊中國菜的博大精深，同時也對簡單的或異國料理感到興趣。

同時，效文也熱愛哈雷機車，我自己從十幾歲開始就很喜愛哈雷。再來就是煙斗，抽著煙斗的人總讓我肅然起敬，這些人各個都是個人物。雖然我早就戒菸，也不會再重拾這個習慣，不過，我曾一度很想擁有一支海泡石煙斗。現在仍會想像著在桌上擺一支耀眼的海泡石煙斗。

效文走遍世界，深入淺出地記錄一路所到過的地方、所遇見的人，各個引人入勝。他也在東南亞進行了許多人道計劃。他在菲律賓巴拉望諸島，協助當地居民建立自給自足、現代化和邁向進步的生活，讓住民從他們自己土地上富饒的資源獲益，也讓他們進而能保護這些資源。

效文對於不同文化的興趣早已超越單純的好奇，而是想探索並托舉著這些文化價值。從效文的字裡行間，我們得以發掘這些文化的共同點，也藉此認識到我們身為人的價值，認識到我們都是平等的。

弗朗西斯科・西奧尼爾・何塞（Francisco Sionil Jose）
知名作家及菲律賓國家文學藝術獎得主

Preface

Twenty books in a series is quite a lot in the same format, especially for an explorer who is always tempted to try something new. So, it is with this notion that I decided to begin a new series of books.

The result is this new pair of books in two different formats. One is smaller, focused more on text and combining both nature and culture, which were separated in the previous series. The other book is larger in format, focused on pictures; a retrospective of the first decade of my photographic career. The former book allows me to focus on the present, while the latter provides me with the leisure to look back and reflect on my past.

Both books are quite personal, but in different ways. I am more thoughtful and journalistic in the first book, and becoming more contemplative, reflective and inward-looking in the second one, bringing context to the content. Both are important for me in my current state of mind and being.

It is my belief that, even while marching forward and breaking new ground, I must also look backward and revisit the path and footprints of where I have come from. Such balance, perhaps in line with the Chinese Ying and Yang cosmology, offers me a stable footing as I walk the remaining steps of my life.

My life has been lived through much toughness in the field, but I have also been most fortunate that I enjoyed and remembered best such moments. I persevered and thrived through difficulties, but I was also blessed with many great friends and supporters. It has been indeed an exciting and sometimes luxurious life to be a career explorer. I hope the pages in both books and this new series will allow me to share special moments and thoughts with my friends, and the public at large.

序

同一系列的二十本書都以一種形式呈現，實在是太多了，尤其是對一位不斷想要嘗試新事物的探險家來說，所以我決定開始著手新的系列。

因此兩本不同風格的作品應運而生。其中一本比較小，以文字敘述為主，結合了自然與文化，以往是將它們分成兩本。而另一本的開本比較大，以照片為主，回顧我第一個十年的攝影生涯。前者讓我能聚焦在現在，後者則讓我輕鬆地回顧過去。

這兩本書對我來說都是非常個人且私密的，但是風格迥異。第一本以較為嚴謹新聞報導的方式呈現，第二本則是我的沉思，我的回顧和內省；我將自己的人生背景帶進書本的內容之中。這兩本書對我現在的心境而言扮演著重要的平衡角色。

我相信，在不斷前進及開闢新天地時，我也應該回過頭看看我過去走過的路，找回自己一路走來的路途和足跡。這樣的平衡或許恰似中國的陰陽宇宙觀，讓我在往後的人生中，每一步都能走得更踏實。

一生在野外經歷過許多磨難，但是也慶幸能樂在其中，留下了最美好的回憶。我走過了重重難關，也很幸運擁有很多好朋友和支持我的人。成為專業的探險家的確讓我的一生充滿刺激，有時也非常享受。希望這兩本書以全新的系列呈現，能讓我把特別的經驗和想法分享給我的朋友和讀者。

目次

UNUSUAL AFFAIR A revolutionary artist and a revolutionary

非比尋常的關係 一位劃時代的藝術家與一位革命家————018

TIBETAN MEDITATION / MEDICINAL INCENSE

靜思與藥用藏香————034

RETRACING THE LONG MARCH IN GUIZHOU on a bicycle

追憶貴州長征 單車記————042

CROSSROAD 十字路口————058

YOUNG MAN AND THE SEA Havana once again

年輕人與海 再訪哈瓦那————072

PEARL HARBOR and USS Hornet, America's first response to aggression

珍珠港大 黃蜂號航空母艦，美國對侵略者的第一個回應————092

EXPLORING UPPER REACHES OF THE CHINWIN RIVER

探索欽敦江的上游————108

MY TAKE ON WILDLIFE PHOTOGRAPHY Winter in Hokkaido

我對野生動物攝影的看法 北海道的冬天————122

MY TOKYO ESCAPADE 我的東京探險————136

HANGZHOU, FORTY YEARS AGO AND NOW

杭州，今昔四十載——————————————150

A PIPE IS NOT all ABOUT SMOKING

煙斗不只用來抽菸而已——————————————166

TO THE SOURCE OF THE BRAHMAPUTRA

布拉瑪普特拉河源頭——————————————182

BACK DOOR INTO BHUTAN Or are we still in China?

從後門進入不丹　還是我們還在中國？——————————————202

CHIANG MAI CAFÉ-RESTAURANTS   And a barber's repertoire

清邁的咖啡餐廳　和一位多技能的理髮師——————————————224

CENTENARIAN PILOT WHO FLEW IN FIVE WARS

From Missionary pilot to Mercenary pilot

參與過五場戰役的百歲飛行員　從傳教飛行員到雇傭兵飛行員——————————————238

OLD HAUNT OF AN OLD HIPPIE

老嬉皮的老地方——————————————262

非
比
尋
常
的
關
係

UNUSUAL
AFFAIRS

Mexico City – September 20, 2016

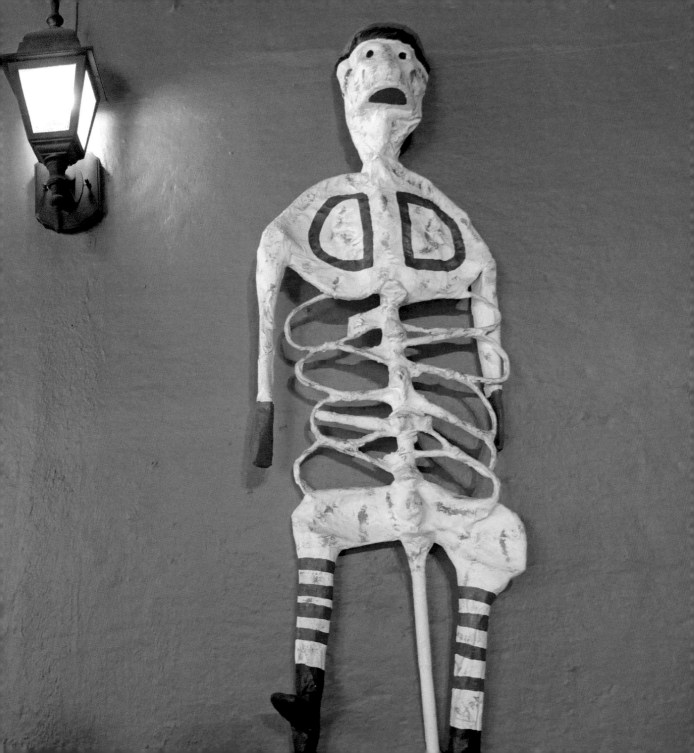

UNUSUAL AFFAIR – A revolutionary artist and a revolutionary

"Who needs feet? I've got wings to fly;" so wrote Frida Kahlo after her right foot had to be amputated in 1953. Indeed, in one of her sketches, there is an image of a person with one leg, rings on the other, and a pair of angel wings. She was to die soon later, in 1954, at a relatively tender and prime age of 47.

As if to further dispel sympathy and to re-enforce her fighting spirit, Frida started fashioning her own costume cum art to accommodate her now changed anatomy. It included a wooden false leg with an elegantly decorated red boot. It came with all the straps for attaching it to her amputated leg.

What surprised me as I looked closely at this piece of art was that the shoe had a colorfully embroidered Chinese dragon on it. Visiting her home studio, a place where Frida Kahlo was born and died, I also saw the toy collection she created, which included some Chinese designs and motifs. These, however, are adaptations of traditional Chinese iconography into her art, like a Ying and Yang emblem on a neck piece. There are other Chinese influences in her life. Her bed faces a horizontal framed picture. On it are, from left to right, portraits of Stalin, Engels, Lenin, Marx, and lastly, that of Mao.

Displayed next to her artificial leg art are two torso corsets, each like a cast. Because of her partially distorted body, crippled after childhood polio and later further complicated by a near-fatal accident on a bus when she was just 18 years old, her physical body was bent out of shape. But her intellectual and artistic mind seems to have hardened. During her lengthy convalescence and recovery, when she was confined to her bed, she painted lying down with a specially made easel. With a mirror set in front of her, she thus began her life-long saga of self-portraits.

She would wear these corsets she made under her clothes in order to hold up her frail body. Two of the corsets on display have graphics on them, including a distinguished one with a red hammer and sickle over the chest. One other corset is so meticulously designed and crafted with leather that it could be worn outwardly, like a decorated piece of armor. Indeed she would use these corsets with her costume, as shown in a self-portrait she made. One particular piece depicted Frida in a leather corset. In the background is a globe with a dove, and an image of Karl Marx with a hand choking the neck of Uncle Sam.

Much of what is now put on display, including paintings, sketches and written text, were recently discovered locked away in an attic and bathrooms of the house. One small painting, surrealistic like many of Kahlo's works, is of a lady laid on a bed, possibly a surgical bed, with anatomy organs including even a snail around her, linked by obviously red blood lines to her womb. This particular work immediately reminded me of an old friend, Zhang Xiaokang, now one of China's best known artists, whom I have known for 30 years, since 1986.

Zhang's bloodline series, most coveted among collectors of modern Chinese art, bear acute resemblance to this particular work by Kahlo. I knew Zhang was an early admirer of surrealism, including works by Bosch. But this piece of work by Kahlo may have given him specific inspiration to start his now famous series.

What sets Frida Kahlo apart from others is perhaps her heritage. Frida's German-Hungarian father provided that strong and disciplined mindset, as well as the Hungarian traits that fueled Frida's Bohemian art design and lifestyle. Her maternal lineage to Mexico provided the other colorful side of her art.

Noting her Jewish background, she preferred to use her name as Frieda but changed it to Frida in the 1930s to disassociate herself from Germany during the Third Reich. An introductory description on the wall to her home/studio museum began with; "Saint, muse, lover, mistress, bisexual, victim and survivor" - Frida was all of that and more.

More, in that her art would transcend her home in Mexico and reach New York's art and social scene, even well into the 21st Century and today. A painting sold in 1938 for USD one hundred would be auctioned off in 2010 for over one million. A surrealistic masterpiece "Two nudes in the forest" went under the hammer this year for 8 Million. Many of her self-portraits also fetched millions.

Frida herself might have been surprised in seeing such prices for her art, bid-up by the power-elite

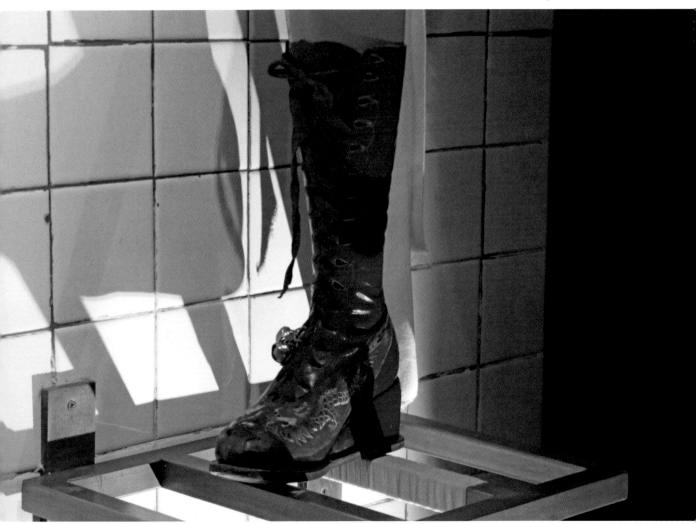

Sketch with wings / 草稿裡的一雙翅膀
Necklace with Ying & Yang / 項鍊上的陰陽
Self-portrait in bed / 臥床自畫像

of the world for her paintings. It was her husband, Diego Rivera, an even more highly regarded artist, who urged the Mexican president to give asylum to Leon Trotsky after he went into exile from the Soviet Union when the revolutionary hero fell out with Stalin. Upon arriving in Mexico in 1937, Trotsky and his wife stayed for two years with Diego and Frida.

That is, until it was discovered that Frida was having an affair with Trotsky. Who seduced who is up to debate, but it is generally believed that Frida had multiple lovers, which drew the jealously of Diego, if they were with men. Frida was also known to have had many female liaisons, which Diego did not seem to mind, until one of those ended up being Diego's younger sister. Such a Bohemian lifestyle of an artist seemed commonplace and even expected during that permissive era. Frida was much admired even among social circles in New York. An excellent painting easel in her studio was a gift from Nelson Rockefeller.

But Frida's affair with Trotsky prompted Diego to ask the couple to leave, and they moved into a high security premises with guard towers a few blocks away. Here Trotsky lived out the remaining year of his life, writing, meeting with his followers from distant lands, and setting the stage for his Fourth International movement.

In May 1940, a first attempt was made on Trotsky's life, as several men made into his guarded house and fired from short range with machine guns into his bedroom. Somehow the couple and their son survived the onslaught by hiding under the bed. Today bullet holes can still be seen on the wall of Trotsky's bedroom. A second attempt by a lone assassin with an ice-axe was successful three months later, and Trotsky died the day after the attack.

Today Leon Trotsky, this famous revolutionary, comrade in arm of Lenin and supreme commander of the Red Army during the Russian revolution, is buried with his wife in the garden of this house, now made into a museum. His fallout with Stalin, which prompted his exile and ultimate assassination, closed a chapter of the revolutionary history of the last century.

The romantic ties of Latin America's most celebrated female artist with a world-renowned revolutionary is only a shadow of the past, separating those growing numbers of people who admire Frida Kahlo's art from those fewer and fewer who continue to follow the dream of an international revolutionary icon.

My visit to these two museums was no doubt the highlight of my return visit to Mexico. I first came here 40 years ago, as a young graduate in Journalism and Art, somewhat of a progressive to radical student, a byproduct of the Vietnam War era. These two museums seem to bring together again my memories of the romanticism of the two disciplines that I had chosen.

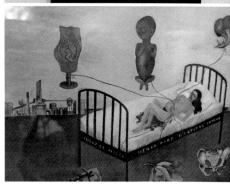

Bed with mirror and portraits /
床前的鏡子和肖像
Leather corset with Marx /
皮製緊身胸衣和馬克斯
Painting with blood lines / 血緣之作

As I boarded the airplane for my flight to Los Angeles, I carried with me over my shoulder a guitar case. Inside was a hand-made guitar from Paracho, a town made famous by all its luthiers, with hundreds of guitar makers, and music shops. I felt like a hippie from 40 years ago. Momentarily, the airline hostess stopped me at the gate and asked, "Did you buy a seat for your instrument?"

"But I am in Business Class and the lady at the counter told me I can carry this onboard," I protested. She went back to the counter and checked. Coming back with my ticket, she gave me a smile, "Ok, Business Class on this flight is not full, you should have room to store it."

For a short moment before she came back, I felt like I was not a hippie, but Yo-yo Ma. He is known to always purchase an extra seat for his Cello. But his is a Stradivarius.

Photo of Frida / 芙烈達留影
Frida's bedside ornaments / 芙烈達床邊的裝飾品
Studio with easel and wheelchair / 畫室中的畫架及輪椅
Corset Costumes / 精緻的緊身胸衣

非比尋常的關係——一位劃時代的藝術家與一位革命家

一九五三年，當芙烈達‧卡蘿（Frida Kahlo）面臨右腳必須被截肢時，她曾這樣寫道：「誰需要雙腳呢？我有一雙能夠翱翔的翅膀。」她的畫稿中的確有這麼一幅畫像，畫中人物只有一隻腳，另一隻腳由圓圈圈組成，背上還有一對天使的翅膀。不久後，芙烈達便於一九五四年離開人世，年僅四十七歲，正值壯年。

彷彿在告訴世人別再對她施捨同情，同時也藉此壯大自己奮鬥的意志力，她開始為自己已改變的身體創作服飾藝術品。其中一件作品是一隻穿著紅色靴子、裝飾高雅的木製義肢，還附上繩帶，好穿戴在被截肢的那條腿上。

仔細一看，我意外地發現靴子上竟繡著一條鮮豔的龍。參訪芙烈達住所的畫室，這個她出生到離世的地方，目睹她一手創作的玩物，其中不乏中國風的設計和主題。芙烈達將這些傳統中國的圖像改變後，再融入自己的創作，例如一條有陰陽圖案的項鍊。從其他地方也能看見中國文化對芙烈達的影響，她的床舖正前面就橫掛著一幅裱框肖像畫，左到右分別是史達林、恩格斯、列寧、馬克思然後是毛澤東。

義肢創作一旁擺放兩件極像鑄鐵的緊身胸衣。由於從小患有小兒麻痺，加上十八歲那年在巴士碰上一場幾乎奪去她性命的車禍，芙烈達的身軀更加變形。但是她的才智與藝術

Trotsky in his study / 書房中的托洛斯基　　　　Trotsky's study / 托洛斯基的書房

天賦卻因此更加茁壯。漫長的修養康復過程，臥床的芙烈達使用特製的畫架作畫。藉由一面擺在面前的鏡子，她開始了此生自畫像的傳奇。

芙烈達穿上這些緊身胸衣來撐起她孱弱的身軀。兩件展出的胸衣上都有圖樣，其中一件的胸口上有一把代表蘇維埃紅色鐵槌及鐮刀，很顯眼。另一件以皮革製作，可以外穿，設計得非常精緻，猶如一件裝飾華麗的盔甲。的確從她的自畫像中可見，芙烈達會將這些胸衣當成服飾一般。有一件作品芙烈達身穿皮製的胸衣，背景還有一個地球和鴿子，以及伸手招住山姆大叔脖子的馬克思畫像。

很多展出的畫作、草稿及書面文字，原本都封存在芙烈達住家的閣樓及浴室中，直到近期才被發現。其中一幅小幅的畫與芙烈達許多作品一樣屬超現實主義，畫中的女子躺在看似手術床上，身旁圍繞著幾個器官解剖圖，甚至還有一隻蝸牛，全部器官都透過血管與床上女子的子宮連接。看到這件作品，我馬上想起一位舊識張曉剛，他是現今中國最為知名的藝術家之一，我從一九八六年就認識他，到現在已經有三十年了。

張曉剛的血緣系列在當代中國藝術收藏家中相當搶手，與芙烈達的這幅畫作頗為神似。據我所知，張曉剛從很早就非常欣賞超現實主義，包含波許的作品。然而，芙烈達的這幅畫或許啟發了張曉剛創作出著名的血緣系列也說不定。

芙烈達之所以與眾不同，或許和她的血統有關。芙烈達遺傳了匈牙利裔德國父親堅強嚴謹的特質，同時匈牙利人的特質展現在芙烈達波西米亞的藝術創作和生活方式。從母親這邊連結到的墨西哥則給予她豐富的色彩。

芙烈達原本將自己的姓氏拼成 Frieda，但因為意識到自己身為猶太人的背景，到了一九三零年代又改回了 Frida，為的是不讓她的姓氏與第三帝國產生聯想。芙烈達故居兼畫室的博物館牆上一段介紹她的文字開頭這樣寫著：「是聖人、是謬思、是愛人、是情婦、是雙性戀、是受害者，也是倖存者。」這些都是芙烈達，但是她不只是如此而已。

不只是如此，芙烈達的藝術品走出了墨西哥，進入紐約的藝術及社交圈，甚至到今日二十一世紀。一九三八年一幅以一百美元售出的芙烈達畫作，到了二零一零年拍賣價已超過一百萬美元。今年，《森林裡的兩個裸體》這幅超現實主義畫作更以八百萬美元拍賣售出，而芙烈達多幅自畫像亦有數百萬美元的價值。

自己的畫作竟會被世界具影響力的菁英競標到這樣的價碼，芙烈達自己可能也會感到不可思議。芙烈達的丈夫迪亞哥‧里維拉（Diego Rivera）是一位更加享譽盛名的藝術家，也正是他強烈建議墨西哥總統提供托洛斯基政治庇護，托洛斯基這位革命英雄因與史達林決裂而出走蘇聯流亡。一九三七年抵達墨西哥後，便與太太在迪亞哥和芙烈

Trotsky's house with guard tower / 托洛斯基設有瞭望塔的住家

Trotsky's tomb / 托洛斯基之墓

達的家中住了兩年。

後來之所以離開，是因為芙烈達與托洛斯基的婚外情東窗事發。而究竟是誰勾引誰，至今仍是個謎，但是據說芙烈達有多位情人，若對象是男性的話，總會讓迪亞哥忌妒。芙烈達也有多位女性的情人，迪亞哥對此倒是不太在意，直到芙烈達最後搭上了他自己的妹妹。如此波西米亞的生活方式在藝術家圈中似乎很常見，甚至在那個開放的年代大家是這樣看待藝術家的。即便在紐約的社交圈，芙烈達仍備受景仰，她的畫室還留有尼爾森·洛克斐勒贈送的高級畫架。

芙烈達與托洛斯基的婚外情促使迪亞哥要求托洛斯基夫婦離開。兩夫婦隨後便搬到幾個街區外一個戒備森嚴、設有瞭望塔的住所。托洛斯基在此寫作、接見遠道而來的追隨者及籌備第四國際運動，並在此度過他的一生。

一九四零年五月，托洛斯基第一次遭遇行刺，幾名男子闖進他戒備森嚴的住處，持著機關槍朝臥房近距離掃射。夫妻倆和兒子躲到床下，幸運地逃過一劫。至今，托洛斯基臥房牆上的彈孔仍清晰可見。三個月後，一名單獨行動的刺客拿著冰斧行刺成功，托洛斯基在遭襲翌日傷重不治。

托洛斯基這位俄國革命期間的著名革命家、列寧身邊的左右手及蘇聯紅軍的總司令，如今與他的夫人長眠在這裡的花園，他的住所也成了博物館。托洛斯基與史達林決裂、流亡，最後遇刺，為上個世紀的革命史畫下句點。

這位拉丁美洲最知名的女藝術家與聞名世界的革命家之間的戀情已成往事，如今仰慕芙烈達藝術的人越來越多，而繼續追隨這位國際革命英雄的人卻越來越少。

參觀這兩座博物館無非是我這趟回到墨西哥最精彩的高潮。四十年前我第一次來到這裡，當年還是一位剛拿到新聞與藝術學位的年輕畢業生，且由於處在越戰年代，是個思想開放甚至激進的學生。這兩座博物館似乎再次讓我想起我所選擇的這兩個領域中所蘊含的浪漫。

登機飛往洛杉磯時，我背著一個吉他盒，裡面裝著一把在墨西哥帕拉丘買的手工吉他，帕拉丘是一個以絃樂器工藝聞名的城鎮，有著數以百計的製琴師及樂器行。此時我像極了四十年前的嬉皮。在登機口空姐把我攔住問：「請問您的樂器有買座位嗎？」

我語帶抗議說：「我搭商務艙，櫃台小姐說可以帶上去。」空姐於是拿著我的機票回到櫃檯確認，回來時，她面帶微笑說：「沒問題，這班的商務艙沒有客滿，應該有空間讓您擺放。」

在空姐離開的片刻中，我覺得比起嬉皮，我更像馬友友，大家都知道馬友友總會為他的大提琴多買機位，但他的琴可是史特拉迪瓦里啊。

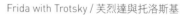

Frida with Trotsky / 芙烈達與托洛斯基

靜思與藥用藏香

TIBETAN MEDITATION
/ MEDICINAL INCENSE

Weixi, Yunnan – October, 2017

TIBETAN MEDITATION / MEDICINAL INCENSE

There are three main types of Tibetan incense. The simplest is for time keeping, usually burning slowly due to the thinner air and lower oxygen on the high plateau, yet perfect as a time keeper since early days. Thus the term, "a stick of incense in time" as a basic unit of calculation. Senior monks may use such incense to mark the time for prayers, or in timing sections when teaching young monks to chant.

Another kind of incense, usually with stronger fragrance, is for environmental purification and cleansing. Among aristocrats and the wealthy with ceremonial costumes, it is normal practice to loan or exchange clothes to maintain diversity. As embroidered clothes cannot be washed, fragrant incense is used to smoke them after use, as a way of cleansing and sterilization.

The most complicated and valuable incense is used for meditation and has medicinal quality, concocted with special Tibetan herbs and medicinal plants. The Tibetan term for such incense is "Sum Bu", "Sum" meaning "sleep well" and "Bu" signifying a long pillar.

Those made in famous monasteries, like the Mindroling monastery in central Tibet, produce a special aroma and have been circulated among Tibetans for centuries. Traditional incense made to these exacting formulas is extremely hard to find and now has become rare and very expensive. It is said to have special qualities for overcoming sleeplessness and insomnia. High monks use such incense also for meditation, and they are of special value as offerings.

Today, due to the huge numbers of Buddhists who patronize Tibetan Buddhism, many brands of Tibetan incense are flooding the market. Some are delivered in very elaborate packaging and sold to the high-end market or to wealthy supplicants. One particular incense lists its ingredients as including powder from musk deer scent pods and pangolin scales; both are products of endangered wildlife that should be under protection.

The CERS collection of Tibetan incense comes from many regions of the plateau. The most unique is that specially prepared by the Luoga Rinpoche, a Living Buddha born in Lijiang in 1964. He was identified at three years old as the 17th reincarnation of the Luoga at Kangguo monastery, his head monastery in Qinghai's Nangchen County. Luoga Rinpoche began his medical study at the age of 14 under the tutelage of a great Tibetan medical master. In 2006 he became the honorary director of the Chinese International Medical Institute.

key ingredients / 主要原料　　Incense base material juniper / 藏香的主要原料杜松　　Variety of Tibetan incense / 藏香系列

Tibetan incense burner / 藏香香檯

CERS has visited the root monastery of Luoga Rinpoche in northwestern Yunnan at the base of the meditation cave of Damozushi, the first Indian sage, or First Master, who brought Buddhism to China. This is where his now famous Tibetan incense is carefully crafted, using an ancient formulation of Tibetan plateau herbs. The most important base is the roots of high altitude juniper, ground into powder. To this are added at least four other scented woods; eaglewood, sandalwood, clove and frankincense.

The packaging is beautifully done in a bark container, with each case holding 108 pieces of select incense, synonymous with 108 volumes of the Kanyur, the most important Tibetan Buddhist sutra, mirrored also in the 108 beads in a Tibetan prayer rosary. Such incense is often called "Wo Xiang", meaning "sleeping incense", as they can be burnt by placing the stick lying down sideways. Special incense boxes, some cast in metal, others constructed of hard wood beautifully painted over, are made for such purpose, to place the incense sideways. It just so happens that the incense is also good for sleeping disorders. It can of course also be burnt upright, and a small ornamental plate is included in the package for this purpose.

This blessed product is in great demand and usually does not reach the market, as almost everything produced is pre-assigned to Buddhist worshippers and monks from Taiwan.

Luoga Rinpoche's monastery below Damozong Cave / 洛噶仁波切的寺院於達摩祖師洞下方

靜思與藥用藏香

藏香主要分為三種。一種用於計時，因為高原上空氣稀薄，氧氣濃度較低，使得藏香燃燒緩慢，從很早以前就是藏人的計時工具，「一柱香的時間」因此成了計時的基本單位。這裡的老僧人會用藏香的燃燒時間來紀錄誦經所需的長短，又或者會在指導年輕僧人誦經時用它來衡量所需的計時。

另一種藏香氣味較為濃烈，多用於淨化環境與清潔。舉例來說，達官顯貴之間經常會出借或交換禮服，以維持服飾的多樣性。但這些刺繡的衣物無法水洗，穿完後就會焚香以煙薰清潔消毒。

其中，製程最為複雜、也最有價值的藏香則用於打坐靜思。這種香具有藥效，使用西藏特殊的草藥和具藥性的植物調製而成。西藏人稱之為「Sum Bu」，「Sum」意指「好眠」，「Bu」代表「長柱」。

著名寺院如西藏中部的敏珠林寺所製的藏香，因為帶有特殊香氣，已在西藏流傳了好幾百年。這些嚴守寺廟古法所製作的藏香因為數量稀少、價格昂貴，如今已極難買到。這種藏香據說還具有治療失眠的功效，高僧打坐時會點上這種藏香，若當成供品則具有特殊意義。

現在信奉藏傳佛教的人口眾多，市面上充斥著琳瑯滿目的藏香品牌，有些包裝極為精緻，專攻高端市場或富有的信眾。其中有一種藏香的原料還標示含有麝香鹿香囊和穿山甲鱗片的粉末，但這兩種動物均已瀕臨絕種，理應設法保育才對。

CERS 收藏的藏香來自青藏高原多個地區，其中最獨特的是由洛噶仁波切特製的藏香。他是一九六四年出生於麗江的活佛，當他三歲時，青海囊謙縣的康果寺認定他為洛噶的第十七世轉世。洛噶仁波切十四歲開始跟著一位西藏醫藥大師習醫，二零零六年當上了中國國際醫學研究院（*Chinese International Medical Institute*）的榮譽院長。

CERS 曾造訪洛噶仁波切在雲南西北的本寺，那裡也正是達摩祖師清修洞穴的所在地，祂是印度第一代祖師，後來將佛教傳入中國。而這裡也正是仁波切知名藏香的研製之地，使用含有青藏高原草藥的古老配方，高山杜松的根是其中最重要的成分，磨成粉後，再加入其他至少四種香木，包括沉香、檀木、丁香及乳香。

每個精緻的木盒裡，都裝有一百零八支嚴選的藏香，如同重要的藏傳佛教經典《大藏經》中共有一百零八冊一樣，而西藏念珠上的一百零八顆珠子也有異曲同工之妙。這類藏香點燃後可以平放，故又稱「臥香」，意即「沉睡的香」，為此也出現了色彩艷麗的特製金屬或硬木香盒，湊巧的是，這種藏香也有療癒失眠的功效。然而臥香也可以直放，因此包裝裡都附有精緻的盤子。

這樣的藏香需求量驚人，產品幾乎沒機會流通到市面上，因為早已被台灣信眾和僧侶預訂一空了。

追憶貴州長征——單車記

RETRACING
THE LONG MARCH
IN GUIZHOU

Guizhou – November 10, 2017

RETRACING THE LONG MARCH IN GUIZHOU *on a bicycle*

The aroma in the air is intoxicating. More so the effect when trying to balance oneself on a bicycle. I take in a deep breath as we are now on a slight incline, climbing uphill on this red asphalt bike way. But the fresh air is permeated with the fragrance of liquor.

This is quite normal, as we are just now going through the wine zone on the outskirt of the ancient town of Moutai, where hundreds, if not thousands, of cellars and liquor distilleries, large and small, are located. Moutai is name of the town but better remembered as the name of the national wine, a white liquor made from sorghum that is served at functions of state in the capital as well as by those who imagine that they can entertain guests as lavishly as at a state dinner. President Trump may still be a bit tipsy, or perhaps hungover, after such a banquet in Beijing a couple days ago.

I first went to China in 1974, two years after Nixon set foot in Beijing. At the time, a bottle of Moutai, which Zhou Enlai offered in a toast to Nixon, might fetch under Rmb50 (USD7.50), a hefty sum when a month's salary for a worker was just about at that level. But it was never really available in the market, as all select items were under quota back then and provided only through rationing, and above all by having the right connections. A bottle of the same vintage today will be

Town at river confluence / 江河匯聚處的小鎮

Mural on village house / 村舍壁畫

under the auctioneer's hammer for upward of USD $4000.

Current production puts a bottle at around Rmb1500 (USD $228) from a peak of Rmb2000 a few years ago when corruption was rampant. It seems ironic that several memoirs of Red Army cadres mention that, while stopping at the town, they used Moutai to rub and nurse their sore legs and feet during the Long March.

We ask at a roadside liquor specialty store for the most noted wine in China, but none is available. The stratospheric price has made the product limited to only the most selective stores. We satisfy ourselves by purchasing a case of six bottles of knock-offs that nonetheless have strong aroma, for a meager Rmb714 (USD $100). At that price, even I can afford to rub my legs after a hard day's work on the pedals.

Less well known is that Moutai the town is the start of a 154-kilometer bicycle path, specially built and sponsored by Moutai liquor to the astronomical amount of USD $600 million. My current trip is an attempt to bike this Long March section. The pavement of the entire route is red in color, concocted by a special mix of asphalt to rep-

resents the Red Army's famed Long March. I however would prefer to think that it is paved with liquor profit to patronize a somewhat vain government about its revolutionary heritage.

The Long March is hailed as the ultimate military maneuver of endurance, as the Red Army retreated from its base in Jiangxi Province in southeastern China to the northwestern Red base of Yenan, with a huge enemy army of Chiang Kai-shek in pursuit and many ensuing battles. The 25,000 Li forced march, 12,500 kilometers, can easily belittle today's ultramarathon or extreme sports.

No wonder that, for a long time in the communist core regime of China, participation in the Long March was considered a stamp of approval to high office, at least until the Cultural Revolution unleashed an unprecedented purge within the Party. But prior to the crucial Central Committee meeting in early 1935 at Zunyi, a town nearby to Moutai, Mao's dominating role within the Party was not secured.

By the time the Long March reached Moutai, Mao's military strategy was largely endorsed and fol-

Painting of Long March / 畫看長征

Team ready go to / 蓄勢待發

lowed by the Red Army. By then Mao had reached this zenith of power with consensus of the Central Committee, rising to a stage of supremacy within the Red Army, after a long period of being sidelined. He led his forces in four crossings of the Chishui River with successive battles that defied the enemy's encircling tactics.

While the breakout was considered by Mao, as well as his admirers, as his most beautiful military maneuver, the much down-played losses and even annihilation of the Red Army ranks was phenomenal. The bicycle route would follow the historic crossings of this particular river all the way to near the confluence with the mighty Yangtze River.

For me however, this bicycle trip is also a test of my own endurance, at a time when I must concede that I am long past my prime in age, though not necessarily in energy, and definitely not in spirit. I also have another agenda, to find out whether two bamboo bicycles made in the Philippines are durable and functional on an extended ride. One of these is actually a folding prototype - only five have ever been produced, each by hand.

My team, seven bikers and three as support personnel, arrived in Moutai after a day and a half of driving from Kunming. We moved into a posh hotel with twenty rooms specially built at the starting point of this over half-bil-

Post mark & hostel / 路標與驛站

Xavier filming / 李伯達拍攝中

Uphill drill / 上坡路段

lion dollar bike path, about four million for each kilometer built. I suddenly felt rather privileged. At dinner, I felt even more privileged when I found out that we were the only guests in the house.

A quick chat with the receptionist revealed that most bikers, few in number and usually only on weekends, are only passing through. Hardly anyone ever stays for the night. Most would take two days to complete the entire route, along which there are fourteen rest stops, including six lodging locations. Each of these hotel/hostels has six to ten guest rooms. A few serious bikers may take just one day to complete the entire 154-kilometer length. My plan is to take three days from start to finish, if my bamboo bikes, as well as my body, hold up.

For the first day of the ride, we took it very leisurely, stopping often to take pictures and rest. Coffee hiatus at the designated rest areas were a joy. Two of my friends, Edward and Ernie, are both of my age group. We all formed a Mutual Admiration Society as we complimented each other about our energy and will power for our age, well north of sixty and barely south of seventy. For me as an explorer it seems quite mundane. But for Edward, a long-time retiree, and Ernie, someone much bound to a desk in the office, it is quite extraordinary.

Our younger team members had far more stamina. Li Na, our Kunming office manager, and Yang Jie, a nurse, each in their colorful mountain bike costumes, would always stop to wait for us. Cao Zhongyu, my long-time driver, would bike back and forth to make sure the seniors in the team were doing alright. Xavier, our CERS filmmaker, would deploy his drone as well as balancing at times on an electric bike to film us in action. The remaining party, Zhang Fan, Wang Jian and Berry Sin

Tucheng street / 土城街坊   Museum re Chishui battles / 赤水之戰博物館

traveled in two vans to intersect with us at various locations where the motor road came along side or occasionally even joined the bike route.

The route along the river was most beautiful and the water of the river very clean. Autumn was setting in, but there were at regular intervals caretakers to sweep up the fallen leaves such that the bike way remained clear. Ms Liu, one of the caretakers, revealed to me that the stretch under her care covers eleven kilometers. She was given a motor-tricycle to enhance her work efficiency, cleaning the road and clearing the trash. Those covering shorter stretches may only use a push tricycle. At every kilometer, a map sign with distance marking would tell the rider where he is within the entire 154-kilometer length. New and clean toilets were also placed at regular intervals along the entire route.

But as policing of the route is slack, we ran into occasional motorcycles and even a few cars and trucks that sneaked in at certain intersections with the road, using the bike route as their short-cut detour from place to place. Such lack of regulatory measures makes it dangerous for riders who assume that they have all right of way throughout the bike route. *Each time these vehicles came up stealthily, we had to get off our bikes to maintain safety. Furthermore, due to a landslide, a stretch of the bikeway was closed and we had to bike on a parallel road with fast motor traffic, making the ride a bit hazardous.*

At the end of the first day, we arrived at a bend of the Chishui River called Red Army Camping Site, a location where the Long March stopped to regroup. By then we had biked 54 kilometers and it seemed a most appropriate place to stop for the night. Getting off the bike to walk upstairs made me feel like the Tin Man in the Wizard of Oz, before his joints received lubrication. But while my legs were just stiff, my butt was in pain, taking a beating from the hard bamboo seat, and there were blisters forming between my toes. That night, from an adjacent room, Edward found out the literal meaning of the term "sound asleep" as he overheard the "sound" part of my sleep.

Miraculously, the next morning, everyone, including three of us seniors, rose to a rejuvenated spirit and seemed ready for the road right after breakfast. But yesterday's last stretch involved a fair amount of uphill gradient which required some serious peddling. By now, two of the bikes had developed some gear problems, reducing them to partial operation with only a few gears.

I had a good look at the map and after consultation with everyone, decided that we should only ride on for another twenty kilometers to just outside the next town, Tucheng. I emphasized that the decision did not mean we would give up on the remaining stretch of the bike path, but would return again to finish up the entire length of the road at a later time.

At 74-kilometer bike marking at the village of Lin Tan, we stopped for a tasty lunch at a local home. Next door was sugarcane field in which locals were making red sugar bricks. I purchased a few bricks as a sweet memory of the pause, but not the end, of my bike journey.

Barely ten kilometers onward is the town of Tucheng where the Red Army suffered a humiliating defeat, nursing its wounds before regrouping to pierce through to an escape route. Looking at the many old houses with a red tag to signify having offered as abode for the communists, the retreating Red Army must have overtaken the entire village. The ancient town is also famous for its liquor, though much eclipsed by the fame of Moutai a hundred kilometers to the south.

As I lay in bed, I thought perhaps this was an appropriate place also for me to nurse the sores on my legs, though not my pride. Another thought crossed my mind, regarding the bamboo bikes I brought all the way from the Philippines to test. These bikes which were conceptualized as a statement regarding the use of sustainable material needed to be developed a bit further.

They cost about USD $1500 each bike, both the Victorian and folding styles. At such hefty prices, few can afford them. In order to be really sustainable and meaningful, as with anything else that catches on this cliché of being eco-friendly, the price must be affordable to most. Otherwise, it would only be an eco-balm to comfort the guilty feelings of those sitting in a comfortable seat. Whereas I must confess, sitting on the bamboo seat on a 74-kilometer ride was not at all comfortable for my rear end.

追憶貴州長征——單車記

空氣中飄著一股令人醺醉的氣味，想穩住腳踏車，卻越感醉意。我們正遇到一段上坡，我深呼吸一口氣，沿著紅色的柏油單車道爬坡而上，清新的空氣中仍瀰漫著酒香。

這並不足為奇，因為我們正騎經茅台古鎮市郊的產酒區，這裡就算沒有成千，也有上百間大小酒窖和酒廠。茅台是鎮名，但大家更為熟知的茅台是一種國酒，一種高粱釀製的白酒，專供國宴使用，因此也有一般人想媲美國宴拿來宴客。幾天前北京國宴剛結束，說不定川普還在微醺甚至宿醉呢！

我在一九七四年首次來到中國，即尼克森訪問中國的兩年後，當時周恩來向尼克森敬酒，喝的就是茅台，當時雖然一瓶不到人民幣 50 元（7.5 美元），卻等同工人一個月的薪水，要價不菲。不過，在那個計劃經濟的年代下，所有名貴的商品只能透過限額配給取得，甚至要有關係才拿得到，當時市面上根本買不到茅台酒。而今天，一瓶七零年代的茅台酒拍賣價可高達四千美元。

因為產量的關係，現在一瓶茅台要價約人民幣 1500 元（228 美元）。幾年前貪污猖獗時，最高曾賣到一瓶人民幣 2000 塊錢。諷刺的是，幾本紅軍幹部的回憶錄都提到，當年軍隊長征停留此地，曾拿茅台酒搓腳消除痠痛。

我們到一家酒品專賣店詢問是否有販售茅台酒，但卻撲了空。茅台因為價格昂貴，只有在少數幾家店才買得到。於是，我們買了一箱六瓶裝的仿製品過過癮，但氣味較嗆，不過一箱才人民幣 714 元（100 美元）而已，這樣的價格，我也可以在騎了一天的車後拿來搓腳。

然而，鮮為人知的是，茅台鎮是一條全長 154 公里自行車道的起點，車道斥資六億美元特別打造，資金來自茅台酒的營收。我這趟要挑戰的就是這個長征路段，整條路線以特殊的紅色柏油鋪成，以象徵紅軍著名的長征。但在我看來，就是一條用酒錢鋪出的車道，拿共產黨輝煌的革命史來討好這個喜歡漂亮的政府。

當年紅軍一路從中國東南的江西省根據地，往西北的延安基地撤退，蔣介石的大批軍隊追趕在後，一路雙方交戰多次。這趟急行軍走過兩萬五千里總長等同於一萬兩千五百公里，可輕易媲美今天的任何一場超級馬拉松或極限運動，長征被譽為考驗耐力的行軍。

也難怪，中國政權核心好一段時間裡，都將是否親歷長征視為進入政府高層任職的指標之一，直至文革大舉清算黨內人士。不過，一九三五年遵義（茅台附近的小鎮）那場關鍵的中央委員會會議之前，毛澤東在黨內的領導地位還沒被確立。

長征隊伍抵達茅台時，毛澤東的軍事策略已獲得多數紅軍的支持與採納，那時，他才取得中央委員會的肯定。毛在沉潛許久後，終於躍上顛峰，聲勢如日中天。他四次領軍勇渡赤水河，在連續幾場戰役中成功化解敵軍的圍剿戰術。

多數仰慕者和毛澤東本人都認為，那次突圍是毛打過最漂亮的一仗，但對於紅軍損失慘重，甚至遭到大舉殲滅，卻輕描淡寫。這條車道正是沿著歷史上四渡赤水的地點前進，一路到赤水河與長江的交會處。

對我來說，這趟單車行也考驗著我的耐力，因為，到了這把年紀，不得不承認體力已開始走下坡了，雖然活力還絲毫未減，精神當然就更不用說了。這次來，還有另一項任務：測試兩部菲律賓的竹製自行車是否耐得住長途騎乘。其中一部還是摺疊式的試作車，目前僅生產五部，每一部都是全手工打造。

我的車隊一行七人，其中三人是支援組。我們從昆明開了一天半的車抵達茅台，入住一家備有二十間客房的高級飯店。飯店就蓋在六億車道的起點（相當每公里四萬美金），讓我突然與有榮焉。吃晚餐時我們才發現，我們是當天唯一一批客人，這讓我更倍感榮幸了。

很快與櫃檯人員聊了一下，原來大多單車騎士（人數其實也不多）僅在周末前來，一般也只是經過，很少人過夜，大部分都選擇兩天騎完全程，沿途更有多達十四個休息站，包括六個投宿點，每一間旅館都有六至十間客房。一些認真的騎士甚至一天就能騎完全程 154 公里。我則計畫三天完成，但前提是竹製車和我的體力要能撐得住。

第一天，我們的步調非常悠閒，不斷停下來拍照休息，到了指定休息區喝上一杯咖啡，真是一大享受。我的兩位隊友 Edward 和 Ernie 年紀都和我差不多，早已過了六十，而離七十也不遠了。我們組成了互濟小組，鼓舞彼此到了這把年紀仍展現的活力和意志力。這次騎乘對我這個探險家來說或許稀鬆平常，但對退休已久的 *Edward* 和坐慣辦公室的 *Ernie* 來說，可就是一大挑戰。

我們年輕隊員的體力要好很多，昆明中心的行政主任李娜和護理人員 *Yang Jie* 不斷停下來等我們，兩人都穿著鮮豔的越野自行車服。長期替我開車的曹中越則騎著車來回穿梭，確保我們這幾個老人沒什麼狀況。CERS 的影片製作人李伯達則邊騎著電動車，邊操控著無人機替我們錄影。另一組人馬包括張帆、王健和 *Berry* 開著兩台休旅車，有時在一般車道，有時在單車道上和我們並行。

沿著河的那一段路，風景最為秀麗，江水無比清澈。雖已漸漸入秋，但仍可見清道夫定期清掃落葉，維持車道的整潔。其中一位清道夫劉女士告訴我，她負責的路段有十一公里，所以配有電動三輪車，才能提高效率把路打掃乾淨。但負責較短路段的人就只有三輪推車。自行車道上每隔一公里，就立有一個路標，標示著距離騎完全程 154 公里的剩餘里程，途中定點設有全新設備且乾淨的廁所。

但因為車道缺乏管制，我們遇過為了抄捷徑而從交叉路口闖進單車道的摩托車，甚至是汽車和卡車。管制如此鬆散，危及單車騎士的安全，而很多騎士也認為自己擁有絕對路權。有車偷闖進來時，我們只能下車步行，以策安全。此外，部分路段因為土石崩塌而封閉，我們被迫併行在車速飛快的馬路旁，十分危險。

第一天結束時，我們來到了赤水河河灣處的一個紅軍駐紮點，當年長征的紅軍曾在此集結軍隊。抵達這裡時，我們已經騎了五十四公里，在此停留過夜看來再適合不過。下車走上樓梯時，我彷彿和綠野仙蹤裡還沒上油的機器人一樣，雙腿僵硬無比。更慘的是在硬竹椅上騎了一天，我的屁股痛得不得了，腳趾也起了水泡。那天晚上，Edward 聽到我「鼾聲如雷」，終於明白什麼叫「睡得香甜」。

不過，隔天早上，包括我們三個老人在內的所有人都奇蹟似地恢復了精神和體力，準備好吃完早餐後立刻上路。只不過，前一天最後一段路程連連上坡，我們踩得用力，目前已有兩台車的零件出現故障，只剩下幾個變速還可以運作。

我拿出地圖研究了一番，和所有人討論後決定，最多只有辦法再騎二十公里，到達下個城鎮（土城）的外圍。我向大家強調，這並不代表我們半途而廢，而是留待下次再回來騎完全程。

最後我們停在了七十四公里處的淋灘村，到當地一戶人家享用美味的午餐。房子旁是一大片甘蔗園，居民將這些甘蔗提煉製成糖磚，我買了一些當作這趟旅程的美好回憶，這次被迫中斷，但我們還會再回來。

不到十公里外就是土城鎮。紅軍曾在這裡兵敗如山倒，但也是在這裡養精蓄銳，重整軍容，最後突出重圍。鎮上許多老房舍門上還掛著紅色牌子，當時供紅軍棲身的地方，想必撤退中的紅軍佔領了整座城鎮。這座古城也以釀酒聞名，只不過名氣遠不如距此南方一百公里的茅台鎮。

我躺在床上心裡想著，這裡或許是我可以好好療癒痠痛的好地方。而那兩部遠從菲律賓帶來測試的竹製車，取竹造車的構想是為了推廣使用環保材料，但看來還有待加強。

這兩台竹製車兼具復古風和折疊功能，各要價 1500 美元上下，一般人實在難以負擔。若想要像其他的知名環保概念品牌一樣永續和普及，價錢就必需親民。否則，只會淪為少數人拿來消除罪惡感的慰藉品罷了。不過，說真的，坐在竹椅上騎乘七十四公里，對我的屁股來說可一點都不慰藉啊。

Ancient town of Tucheng / 土城古鎮

十字路口

CROSSROAD

Playa del Carmen, Mexico – November 30, 2017

CROSSROAD

"I am at a crossroad," we often hear people saying about certain turning points in their lives. But for me, everyday I'm at a crossroad, be it literally or figuratively. I cross the street, I come across people, mundane or special, things cross my mind, what to eat and what to buy, who to call, where to go, or what to Google.

So currently, I'm at the crossroad from North America to Latin America. The Caribbean Sea is only a block away. Miami and Cuba, a finger-stretching distance on a map, is within an hour's plane ride. For the last week, I have been driving around the Yucatan Peninsula of Mexico. The last time I was here, in 1975, I was barely 25 years old, as I drove through on my way from Canada to South America.

Edward, the same friend who drove with me in 1975 in a VW camper van, is again with me. While both of us are closing on 70, our exploration spirit has remained as vital as our youthful days, though our energy can hardly match those days, when our eyes would turn upon seeing women our same age passing by along the sandy white beaches of this beautiful coastline. Today we may still cast our eyes, but not on women our same age!

1975 HM & Ed escapade / 一九七五年 HM 和 Edward

It seems with China's opening up and all the young and educated Chinese roaming the world, Mexico and Yucatan should enjoy a proportionally fair share of this new tourist influx. But it is not the case. I saw in ten days of my time on the peninsula no more than a dozen or so Chinese tourists. Apparently, shopping meccas of the world, like London, Paris and Milan, are still much higher on their list.

In those days, we did our research in university libraries and scoured through the few books available to study these places before setting foot on the ground. Today, all this knowledge and information is at everyone's fingertips, within easy reach of our mobile phones. But I must say, compared to forty years ago, the joy of surprise and discovery is far diluted in today's internet world. People roam the world not in pursuit of knowledge or curiosity, but just for the experience, worse still for shopping, or bragging rights.

Today Mexico is a different scene. The Gringos are still flooding in, but many are capable of speaking Spanish, as they are likely from the lower US states like Texas, Florida or California. Mayan ruins that we once scaled to the

Hacienda entrance / 莊園入口

top to observe a sunrise or sunset are off limits to foot traffic now. The base of the pyramids is all roped off, as far too many tourists' feet could soon wear out the hardest of rocks. And the danger of someone falling from these heights is real, not imagined.

We flew from Los Angeles into Cancun in the northeastern corner of the Yucatan Peninsula. From there we began our drive around the entire peninsula, stopping at some of the important archaeological sites as well as coastal and inland towns. People in rural Yucatan live a very basic life. There seems far more land than people, as much of the low growth jungle remains undeveloped. Farms are few and far apart.

At Merida, an ancient town slightly inland, we stayed at a hacienda. Colonial Spain still filled the air due to the vibrant color on the building, with decorative stained-glass windows and doors to match. The town center is still full of activities, though tourists are few. As with most Mexican towns, the cathedral is at its center, and thus a center of activities, both religious and civil. A small university is housed in an old traditional building nearby. A few horse-drawn carriages may be the only scene that seems touristy; the rest of the place is extremely local.

We visited three ruin sites of the Mayan people. At each place, we paid for ad-

mission, like visiting any amusement park or museum. But it seems strange that the first site of Chichen Itza has scores of venders inside the ground, with stores selling colorful knick-knacks, whereas at Uxmal, not one vender can be seen inside the site. Perhaps such archaeological facilities are managed by dramatically different departments or department chiefs.

At a third site by the coast in Tumal, the last Mayan site to be built and abandoned in the 1500s, and the only site directly next to the sea, there are no shops inside the grounds. But here tourists are allowed to go by some wooden stairs down to a beach, and swim right in the turquoise blue sea under the cliff, with the gods watching from the ruins above. While humans are prohibited from setting foot inside the stone structures, the iguanas (a lizard of Central America), large and small, plenty of them, are having a field day all over these ruins.

Near the end of this ten-day 1500-kilometer journey, I drive into the village of Xcalak next to the small coastal town of Mahahual where Mexico and Belize border each other. The world's second largest barrier reef is just across the border in Belize. Most tourists come here for the white sandy beach, and for diving or snorkeling. I, on the other hand, am interested in the furthest border town of Mexico.

Merida churches / 梅里達的教堂 　　University at Merida / 梅里達的大學 　　University courtyard / 大學中庭

Both Xcalak and Mahahual used to be fishing villages, but the latter has since turned into a tourist destination. While there are many small hotels and restaurants in Mahahual, fifty kilometers away Xcalak has not one hotel for guests, with its meager population of 300 inhabitants. At the time of my visit, I cannot even find a joint for a meal. A tiny lighthouse is the only landmark, though it is across the border in San Pedro of Belize. That is one of the most popular diving spots in the world.

I was tempted to find a boat to sail across the border into Belize. After all, it has been ten days of struggling to get around with my most rudimentary few words in Spanish, drawn from a vocabulary I last used 42 years ago when I first traveled through Central and South America with a pocket dictionary. Whereas Belize is a former British colony and English is spoken.

But my time in Mexico is coming to an end, and Belize has to wait. After all, my memory of Belize from some 40 years ago is still nostalgic. And with almost all places I revisit these days after decades of being away, the memory of the past is far more romantic than today. The same young women I laid my eyes on in 1975 would be sporting gray and white hair like myself if I were to run into them again. At this particular crossroad, I opt for a U-turn.

HM sitting top of pyramid / HM 攝於金字塔

十字路口

常常聽到正處在人生轉捩點的人說：「我來到了人生的十字路口。」但是對我來說，我每天都在十字路口面臨選擇，不論是按照字面上的意思或是比喻上的用法。我過馬路、我遇見人、平凡或特別的人、我思考著要吃什麼、買什麼、要打給誰、要去哪或要 *Google* 什麼。

好比現在，我就正在北美前往拉丁美洲的十字路口上。加勒比海就在不遠處，而邁阿密和古巴在地圖上也只是一根手指頭的距離，還不到一小時的飛行時間。這一個禮拜我開車繞著墨西哥的猶加敦半島跑，上一次來到這裡是一九七五年的事了，那時我還是個不到二十五歲的年輕人，正從加拿大開著車往南美前進。

一九七五年和我一起開著福斯露營車的好友 *Edward* 這次又再度與我同行。如今我們都年近七十，體力大不如前，但是我們探險的精神依舊高昂，如同年輕的時候。當年我們的眼睛會被在這美麗白沙灘上的同齡小姐所吸引；如今我們的視線還是會被吸引，却不是被同齡的女士所吸引。

隨著中國的開放，年輕一代受過教育的中國人開始走向世界各地，墨西哥和猶加敦理應能看到這樣一批的中國觀光客，但是並沒有。我停留在猶加敦半島這十天裡，只見到約略十多位中國遊客。顯然像倫敦、巴黎和米蘭這些購物聖地還是排列在他們觀光地的前幾名。

當年要出發前，我們必須到大學圖書館翻出僅有的幾本書，仔細地研究要去的幾個地方。如今，這些知識和資訊只要手機一滑就能找到。但是我必須說，與四十年前相比，在網路時代已經沒有那種發現的驚喜和喜悅了。現代人走向世界，不再是為了追求知識或滿足好奇心，而只是想要體驗，更糟的是只是為了購物，或只是為了吹牛。

如今的墨西哥已經大不相同。這些英語系的老外持續湧入，而其中有不少人是會講西班牙語的，他們多來自德州、佛羅里達或加州這些美國南部的州。我們曾登頂望日出賞夕陽的馬雅遺跡，如今已經禁止遊客進入。金字塔下面也圍起封鎖線，因為遊客真的太多了，再堅硬的岩石也會磨損。這樣的金字塔真的有可能讓人失足而栽下去。

我們從洛杉磯飛往猶加敦半島東北角的坎昆，再從坎昆開車環整個半島，途中參訪一些重要的考古地點，還有一些沿海與內陸的城鎮。猶加敦鄉下過的生活仍然非常簡樸。這裡地廣人稀，大多的矮叢林還沒有被開發。農地很少，而且彼此的距離也很遠。

我們繼續往內陸前進來到了梅里達這座古鎮，並停留在一間農莊。這裡充滿西班牙殖民的氣氛，建築色彩豐富，門窗都有彩繪玻璃。市中心充滿活力，但是遊客卻不多。梅里達與多數的墨西哥城鎮一樣，以大教堂為中心，一切活動都圍繞著它，不管是宗教的還是民間的。有一所小型的大學就座落在教堂附近的老建築裡。這裡有幾個馬車是唯一看起來跟觀光有關的，其他地方仍然非常本土。

Ruins by the sea at Tumal / Tumal 海岸遺跡一景
Uxmal pyramid / 烏斯馬爾的金字塔

我們參訪了三處馬雅遺址。每個地方都要付費入場，就像去任何遊樂園或博物館一樣。但耐人尋味的是，我們的第一站奇琴伊察古城裡面有不少販賣小飾品的攤販，而在烏斯馬爾卻一家也沒看到。或許是因為這些考古園區是由完全不一樣的部門或主管負責管理的關係。

第三站，我們來到了海岸邊的 Tumal，是馬雅人興建的最後一座城鎮，約在一五零零年遭到遺棄，也是唯一一座緊鄰海邊的遺跡，裡面不見一家商店。但是在這裡觀光客可以沿著木梯走到海灘，在遺址裡眾神的觀望之下，敞伴在峭壁下湛藍的大海裡游泳。雖然人們不能隨意地進入石牆內的遺址，但是美洲鬣蜥（一種中美洲蜥蜴），大大小小，為數眾多，卻能在其中自在遊走。

十天，一千五百公里的旅程將接近尾聲，我開著車進到了 Xcalak，這個村子緊鄰墨西哥與貝里斯邊境的海岸小鎮瑪哈威。全世界第二大的堡礁就位在跨過貝里斯邊境的外海，潔淨的白色沙灘吸引很多觀光客來這裡潛水或浮潛，然而我感興趣的是墨西哥邊境最遠的城鎮。

Mayan old look / 傳統馬雅人的樣貌
Mayan face relief / 馬雅浮雕
Mexican new face / 墨西哥新面孔

Xcalak 和瑪哈威曾經都是漁村，但是瑪哈威後來卻成了觀光勝地。小旅館、小餐館林立，但是五十公里外的 Xcalak 卻不見一間旅館，這裡人口只有三百人。我來的時候，甚至還找不到一家餐館吃飯。小燈塔是唯一的地標，而且還位在貝里斯邊境的聖佩德羅。而這裡是全世界最受歡迎的潛水地點之一。

我本來想找艘船跨過邊界到貝里斯。畢竟十天的行程裡，我只能用我極為粗淺的西班牙語和人打交道，而且這些還是從四十二年前第一次來到中南美洲時用的口袋字典學來的。貝里斯曾是英國殖民地，所以他們說英語。

只不過，我的墨西哥行必須在此打住，貝里斯是就留待下次吧。畢竟記憶中四十年前的貝里斯還是很令我懷念。這次我再訪闊別了幾十年的地方，都已經不如過去記憶中的那樣浪漫。如果還能遇見一九七五年那些吸引我目光的小姐們，她們或許已經和我一樣白髮蒼蒼。在這個十字路口上，我，選擇掉頭。

年輕人與海

YOUNG MAN
AND THE SEA

Havana, Cuba – Dec 5, 2017

YOUNG MAN AND THE SEA
Havana once again

"Here, Take Five please," I said as I handed over five Cuban One Peso coins to Aliosca, the young pianist with curly hair. He looked down momentarily at his hand full of coins, thanked me, and began playing Besame Mucho, the popular Latin song with his own jazz improvisation, followed by Malaguena, again with a jazz bend to it.

But I wanted "Take Five," the jazz number made famous by Dave Brubeck and his Quartet. So be it, I should not insist, given that most of Aliosca's scores are jazz renditions of good, familiar choices. Unlike outside on the street of Obispo, this busiest walking street of Old Town Havana, where street musicians or restaurant quartets are all playing to the rhythm of rumba music.

The last time I stayed at the Hotel Florida, it was a well-dressed young lady behind the piano playing classical. Aliosca must be quite new at the scene. No wonder Emma, the young lady attending at the bar who mixed my Mojito, does not even know his name. Neither does the man waiting table.

All fine hotels are owned and operated by the government, and there seems to be a regular turnover in staff, perhaps based on who is in favor and who is falling out of favor, filling such prime and plum jobs. Tipping by tourists can quickly become multiple times a person's regular salary.

There are more tourists around Havana's old town. Likewise, hotels and restaurants are far more abundant, compared to ten years ago, or even three years ago. There are even many home stay places coming up, helping a budding private sector to move away from state planned economy. The changes over my four visits is quite obvious, though I heard the peak had come and gone right after Obama's visit and the lifting of sanctions on the island country. By the waterfront, I saw two huge cruise ships docking within two days, pouring large groups of tourists into the streets.

Cars from the 1950s, Chevrolet, Cadillac, Oldsmobile, Buick, Chrysler, Dodge, Ford and even a few Thunderbirds and Studebakers, are now more polished and remain a frequent retro-scene around town. These cars have become the most impressive and dramatic icons of Cuba, taking visitors into a nostalgic past.

This is further complemented by street blocks of architectural façade from the same era, with grand columns, marble floors and staircases. But so many of these are dilapidated, some barely standing, with exception of those

Aliosca on the piano /Aliosca 的鋼琴演奏　　　　　Emma the bartender / 調酒師 Emma　　　　　Hotel Florida / 佛羅里達酒店

around the center of tourist activities, which are well restored.

Gaudi single-handedly upheld the tourist gift shops in Barcelona. The parallels here in Cuba are images of Castro and Che Guevara, highly commercialized into tourist memorabilia, while reminding everyone of the country's revolutionary past. Even Professor Escobar, a medical doctor, self-taught himself in art and took up a stand at the weekend art market boulevard.

I tried to revisit the cigar factory near the capital building. The four-story, orange building is still standing. But the factory that charmed tourists for years has closed and moved further outside of town. The shop at the entrance is, however, still open to shoppers eager to purchase the famed cigars, authentic and at reasonable prices, avoiding the contraband, often cheaper copies and fakes, on offer next door or on any backstreet.

I opted for two boxes, each with 25 cigars individually packed in beautiful aluminum cases. Romeo y Julieta is said to have been a favorite of Churchill, though at Grande size. Punch is not as well-known. But I chose it for its military dark green aluminum casing. They may come in handy as great gifts, one at a time, to smoking connoisseur friends.

While paying for the cigars, I thought of my friend David Tang who passed away recently. David was long-time Asia agent for these fine cigars. He offered me a full box of Cohiba as a parting gift, opened and with only one cigar missing. This was after we enjoyed a simple breakfast together at his home. I sat and ate at a small table next to his bed, whereas he was enjoying his coffee in bed. I used to pick up my passport with a Cuban visa at his home, date left blank for me to fill in. David being the Honor-ary Counsel of Cuba.

I visited 86-year-old Ho Chiu-lan in Chinatown. Chiu-lan was born Cuban but was adopted by a Chinese when three years old. CERS invited her and her friend Wong Mei-yuk to Hong Kong three years ago to enjoy Cantonese opera while making a documentary film about her past as a lead opera performer in old Cuba Chinatown. The film was later shown on Cathay Pacific long-haul flights to commemorate the airline's 70th anniversary.

"Today there may be less than 100 Chinese remaining here in Havana," Chiu-lan said with a tone of sadness. At its prime, Cuba had over 400,000 Chinese and Havana was home to half of that total, being the largest concentra-tion of overseas Chinese in north America. Chiu-lan acted in one of the four professional Cantonese opera troupes of Havana. Today Chiu-lan is very eager to find a way to send her grandson, a quarter blood Chinese, to China for university study.

Chong-jai (Singing Boy) today is 25 years old and works as sort of a laborer. But he has been keen in learning Chi-nese, as well as English. At the Chinese Beneficence Society downstairs of Chiu-lan's home, Chong-jai is the lead drummer for the Lion Dance Troupe. As this was a Saturday, young kids were around to learn Lion Dance and martial art. Chong-jai did not hesitate to bring out the drum and played several numbers as accompaniment to the young lions. On the weekend, he also taught children how to play the drum.

With his directness and the progress in language study since I met him three years ago, I promised to assist him in gaining entry into a Chinese University and support his studies in the Orient. I am sure this opportunity would

Cruise Ship with old car / 遊輪與古董車
Retro but real / 復古，但是是真的

allow the young man a turning point in life. With luck he may even become a future connection of Cuba to China.

I stopped by the huge art market at an old pier turned into shops. Carlos Ongal is an art teacher but set up a stand here to peddle his paintings. While most pseudo artists copy multiple duplicates of paintings with the same theme of Havana with vintage cars or other pop art, Carlos does landscape originals. I particularly appreciate a large piece of an autumn forest with water reflection on the ground. It was quickly taken off its frame and rolled up as part of my luggage.

Through introduction of a friend in Hong Kong, I met Daniel Torres and wife Alina. At 47, Daniel has multiple degrees including a doctorate in Conservation of Cultural Heritage. His wife is a biologist turned museum studies. Both are formerly speleologists though working in different universities. This background strikes a common chord with CERS with our own caving team and study of karst.

Furthermore, Daniel's archaeological excavation history spans 27 years since he first graduated from university. More recently he has gotten multiple ratings for his diving license in order to expand his focus to marine archaeology of sunken ships. One such project focused on trying to relocate a wooden boat *purportedly from a thousand years ago, once discovered by a former President of the Cuban Speleological Society in 1950, but since buried under the sand on the beach.*

The husband and wife team have worked with an isolated and insulated community in the eastern tip of Cuba for over two decades. Daniel leads his students on two field expeditions each year to excavate and organize data at this remote village. But this year only one trip was made as they fell short of traveling money for the students. CERS came just in time to offer that modest sum to assist them.

Daniel found out that I was once a National Geographic journalist, though that stint was from over thirty years ago when the magazine was at its prime. Somehow with that magazine, it is like an old coin that still shines a bit and carries some worth as credential. Today, that yellow border frame shines more as a brand name, quite empty inside, just like its logo. No doubt it has to be sold to a commercial entity. I hope it would not become like Cinderella's vain stepmother, looking into her mirror. Daniel lamented his own rather disappointing experience with the National Geographic. His award as a young explorer in 2012 was forfeited when National Geographic reasoned that US Treasury sanction prohibited dispersing his prize money.

Street art vender / 藝術品攤販

Girl at play / 遊戲中的女孩

Dr Escobar / Escobar 博士

While two grants were promised, he went ahead and did the field expeditions of excavation and follow-up work on archaeology in eastern Cuba. Even executive personnel from National Geographic visited him on site. But the promised sum never arrived. When he asked, they listed very tough conditions, including citing US sanction regulations as well as demand for him to give up all rights to his research material and results, which he declined to do for the integrity of his country and himself. As I often say, "intellectual property" is not very intellectual when organizations make demands to commercialize or monopolize it.

I feel gratified that CERS, being as small as we are, can afford to support individuals based on trust, just like myself being the beneficiary of many individual friends and patrons who had supported me over long years. Large organizations perhaps need to put in place a system to manage the huge amount of applications and reporting paperwork, budgets and accounting mechanisms, often making such dealings become extremely impersonal and bureaucratic. While many philanthropists are well educated, respectable, and at times even humble, not a few of the administrators controlling the purse string of foundations and donors are arrogant, dispersing support as if giving hand-outs to even the most worthy recipients. Big organizations invest in paper and numbers, small ones invest in personal relationship and trust.

Our response to Daniel's need at our first meeting with an immediate decision to help is one such example. It contrasts the approach of our 30 years old organization to that of a world-famous 130 years old institution. Daniel and wife parted with me after a short lunch, but I look forward to inviting them to some of our sites in Asia before too long, as we begin to extend our collaboration *beyond just assisting their students on an upcoming field trip.*

Momentarily, my mind is drawn to Hemingway's Old Man and the Sea. Though the marlin was a great catch, with too many sharks around, before the Old Man could reach shore, all that was left of the marlin was its bones. Daniel is a young man, and it takes just a small organization like CERS to support his work. He does not need to catch a big fish in an ocean full of sharks.

Coffee over dilapidated house / 破屋中喝咖啡

年輕人與海 再訪哈瓦那

「請來個 *Take Five* 吧！」我邊說，邊掏出 5 個古巴比索硬幣給 *Aliosca*，這位一頭捲髮的年輕鋼琴師。他看了一下手中的五個銅板，向我道謝，開始彈奏拉丁名曲 *Bésame Mucho*，融入了他自己即興的爵士風，接著彈 *Malagueña*，同樣也加進了爵士。

但是我想要聽的是「*Take Five*」啊，那首戴夫・布魯貝克和他的四重奏樂團最出名的爵士曲目。算了吧，我不堅持了，何況 *Aliosca* 改編的大部分都是耳熟能詳的經典爵士樂曲。不同於奧比斯保的街道，這條哈瓦那舊城繁忙的街道上，不論是街頭音樂家或是餐廳裡的四重奏樂團，演奏的都是倫巴。

上次來到古巴我住在佛羅里達酒店，鋼琴師是一位穿著端莊的年輕女士，彈著古典音樂。*Aliosca* 應該是新來的，也難怪在酒吧替我調著莫希托的年輕女士 *Emma* 不知道他的名字。連服務生也不曉得。

這裡所有的高級飯店都是屬於政府並由官方經營的，員工流動頻繁，極有可能是看受不受歡迎來決定。尤其這些搶手的職缺，遊客給的小費有可能是他們底薪的好幾倍。

與十年前或甚至三年前相比，哈瓦那舊城區的遊客越來越多，飯店餐廳的數量也隨之增加，甚至出現很多像民宿這樣的地方，私營產業逐漸茁壯，似乎開始擺脫國家計劃經濟的束縛了。我來了古巴四次，每次都可以感受到明顯地改變，儘管聽說在歐巴馬到訪及解除對這島國的制裁後，人潮的高峰來了也退了。兩天內我看到兩艘大遊輪停靠，把帶來的觀光客往街道裡倒。

一九五零年代的車，雪佛蘭、凱迪拉克、奧斯摩比、別克、克萊斯勒、道奇、福特，甚至還有幾輛雷鳥和斯圖貝克，在這裡都被保養的都非常好，是城裡常見的復古景象。這些古董車成為古巴最令人印象深刻，也最能代表古巴的市容景觀，它們帶著遊客回到令人懷念的過去。

街道建築物的外觀也是採用同一時期的風格，雄偉的樑柱、大理石地板和樓梯，完美地襯托著街景。然而，許多建築物已經年久失修，有些甚至搖搖欲墜，只有在旅客聚集區域裡，老建築才被妥善照顧與修復。

A posh theme hotel / 高級主題飯店　　　　　　　　　　Cat on old street / 老街上的貓

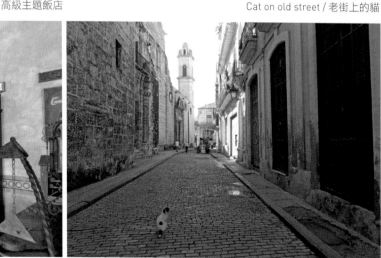

相較於高地一個人就支撐起巴塞隆納的觀光禮品店，古巴則是將卡斯楚和格瓦拉的形象高度商業化，以紀念品的形式，不斷提醒著大家這個國家的革命史。甚至是身為醫生的 Escobar 教授，除了自學藝術外，到了週末也會到藝術市集擺攤。

我試圖再去國會大廈附近的一間雪茄工廠。橘色外牆的四層樓建築還在，但是昔日吸引大批觀光客的製菸廠已然關閉，遷到了郊外。不過入口處的商店還開著，讓顧客可以買到貨真價實的著名雪茄，而不是在隔壁或是巷弄裡販賣的廉價仿冒品。

我選了兩盒，各二十五根，每一根都裝在精美的鋁管裡。據說，邱吉爾最喜愛特大支的 Romeo y Julieta。而 Punch 就沒有那麼出名，但是因為它軍綠色的鋁管包裝，所以我還是選了 Punch。剛好可以當成禮物送給對雪茄講究的朋友，一次送一支。

結帳時，我突然想起最近過世的一位友人鄧永鏘。他長期在亞洲代理這些高級的雪茄。他曾經送我一大盒高希霸雪茄當作臨別贈禮，但是盒子已經開過了，裡面還少了一支。送我雪茄之前，我在他家和他一起享用一頓簡單的早餐。我坐在他床邊的一張小桌子吃著早點，鄧永鏘則躺在床上享用他的咖啡。以往我都會到他家拿我的古巴簽證，簽證上的日期欄都是空白的，好讓我自己填寫。因為鄧永鏘他是古巴駐香港的名譽領事。

這次回來，我也到唐人街探望八十六歲的何秋蘭女士。秋蘭在古巴出生，三歲時被一位中國人收養。三年前，CERS 曾邀請秋蘭和她的好友黃美玉到香港欣賞粵劇，同時也替秋蘭拍了一部紀錄片，關於她過去在古巴舊唐人街劇場當粵劇主角的歷史。後來國泰航

Old new & broken / 老屋、新屋、破屋

空七十周年慶的時候，也在長途班機上播放了這部影片。

「現在還住在哈瓦那的華人可能還不到一百人。」秋蘭語帶悲傷地說。全盛時期，古巴曾經有超過四十萬華人，光哈瓦那就有二十萬，是當時北美華僑密度最高的地方。秋蘭曾在哈瓦那四個職業粵劇團中的其中一團演出。現在，她非常希望能把她那個擁有四分之一華人血統的孫子送到中國讀大學。

Chong-jai（歌唱的男孩）今年二十五歲，算是一名工人。但是他很熱衷學習中文和英文。華人慈善會（*Chinese Beneficence Society*）就在秋蘭家的樓下，*Chong-jai* 是這裡舞獅團的首席鼓手。那天剛好是星期六，小朋友們來學習舞獅和武術。*Chong-jai* 俐落地搬出鼓來，打上幾輪，為小獅子配樂。他也會利用週末教小朋友打鼓。

三年前我見過 *Chong-jai*，他的語言進步了不少，為人坦率，我答應會協助他申請進入中國的大學就讀，並且幫助他在東方的學業。我相信這個機會是這位年輕人人生中一個重要的轉捩點。若有幸，他日後或許會成為古巴和中國間重要的橋樑。

我去了一個由舊碼頭改建，佔地廣闊的藝術市集。*Carlos Ongal* 是位美術老師，也在這裡設攤販售自己的畫作。很多偽藝術家只會複製，千遍一律的哈瓦那古董車或其他流行藝術，但是 *Carlos* 的作品都是獨創的風景畫。我特別喜歡其中一幅大版面的作品，畫的是秋季的森林，地上的水反射著倒影。這個作品很快地從畫框被拿下來，捲好，成為我行李的一部份。

Chong-jai sings for grandma / Chong-jai 為祖母高歌
Drum for Lion Dance / 醒獅擊鼓
Weekend learning / 週末學藝

透過香港友人的介紹，我結識了 *Daniel Torres* 和他的夫人 *Alina*。四十七歲的 *Daniel* 擁有許多學位，包括保存文化遺產的博士學位。*Alina* 原本是生物學家，後來鑽研博物館研究。夫妻倆都曾經是洞窟學者，但在不同大學任職。這樣的背景恰好與 *CERS* 不謀而合，因為我們自己也有探洞及研究石灰岩的團隊。

此外，*Daniel* 大學畢業後便開始從事考古工作，已經二十七年了。最近，他拿到了幾個不同級別的潛水證，準備將他的考古研究擴大到在海洋的沉船。而其中一個項目就是試圖找到一艘據說有千年歷史的木造船，這艘船在一九五零年曾被古巴探洞學會（*Cuban Speleological Society*）的前會長發現，但是之後就被海沙淹沒。

這對夫妻檔和古巴東部一個偏遠的社區合作超過二十年。*Daniel* 固定每年會帶學生到這個偏遠的村落從事實地考察兩次，一邊挖掘，一邊整理這村落的資料。但是今年由於給學生的經費短缺，他們只去了一次。*CERS* 及時出了點棉薄之力贊助他們。

Busy Obispo street / 奧比斯保繁忙的街道
Old meets modern / 復古遇上現代
Street performers / 街頭藝人

Daniel 後來得知我曾經在美國的《國家地理雜誌》擔任記者，但已經是三十年幾年前的事了，當時正值該雜誌的全盛時期。不知何故，這本雜誌好像個舊硬幣，閃爍著一點光芒，還有些公信力。如今，那個黃色外框的品牌更加耀眼，但是就像那個商標一樣，裡面空無一物。無疑地它已經被營利事業收購。我希望它不會變成灰姑娘裡那個虛榮的後母，只會望著鏡子裡的自己。*Daniel* 感嘆他與美國《國家地理雜誌》的合作經驗。他在二零一二年以年輕探險家的身分獲獎，但獎項卻遭沒收，雜誌社給的理由是，美國財政部依據制裁法令禁止發放這筆獎金。

獲得兩筆承諾會發放的款項，*Daniel* 動身前往古巴東部，進行實地考古挖掘和後續的工作。美國《國家地理雜誌》甚至還派了高層到現場訪問他。但事後發現，承諾的款項都沒有實現。*Daniel* 前去詢問，對方卻列出極為嚴格的條件，包括引用美國制裁的規定，甚至要求他讓出研究資料和研究成果。為了捍衛國家和自己的尊嚴，*Daniel* 斷然拒絕。我常說，組織機構想要佔有或藉「智慧財產」來

賺錢或獨佔時，就沒那麼有智慧了。

我很欣賞 CERS 的規模雖小，但卻能以信任為基礎去協助他人，就像我自己一樣，多年來有許多朋友和贊助者支持我。大型組織或許因為需要一套制度來管理龐大的申請文件、報告、預算及會計，但是互動變得僵化也官僚。儘管很多慈善家都受過很好的教育、德高望重，甚至也很謙虛，但還是有不少基金會的經費管理人和捐贈者態度高傲，給予捐助時好像是在施捨別人，即使給予的對象是最恰當的人選。大型的組織投資在紙張和數字，小型的組織投資在人與人之間的情誼和信任。

CERS 就是這樣的例子，與 Daniel 第一次會面後，我們立刻決定協助他。這正也就能看出一個三十歲的組織和一個一百三十歲聞名世界機構的差異。Daniel 和他太太與我吃過簡短的午餐後向我道別，不過我期待不久後能邀請他們來參訪我們在亞洲的幾個基地，因為除了協助他們學生未來的實地考察外，我們也開始展開更進一步的合作。

我心中頓時浮現海明威的《老人與海》。捕到了馬林魚雖然算是豐收，但是水中有太多的鯊魚環伺，老人在靠岸前，馬林魚早被吃得只剩下骨頭。Daniel 還年輕，像 CERS 這樣的小組織可以支持他。他大可不必在滿是鯊魚的海裡捕撈大魚。

Young man and the sea / 年輕人與海

珍
珠
港

PEARL HARBOR

Alameda, California – December 7, 2017

PEARL HARBOR
and USS Hornet, America's first response to aggression

"We apologize with profound respect and condolences on behalf of the people and government of Japan to those who lost their lives in the war." So began Jun Yamada, Japanese Consul General in San Francisco. Yamada was introduced as the first speaker on a stage in front of a huge American flag, inside the hangar of the aircraft carrier USS Hornet.

This is a special day, not just any day, on the USS Hornet which is moored next to a pier in Alameda inside San Francisco Bay, open to the public as a naval relic of the past. On this day seventy-six years ago, Japan's Imperial Army struck Pearl Harbor and inflicted devastating destruction to the US Pacific fleet.

As the group listened, Consul General Yamada continued to expand on the reconciliation process and praised America for assisting Japan after the War. He bears the same name as the notorious general who commanded Unit 731 in Manchuria, which experimented on humans with biological and chemical weapons during WWII.

Listening on the sidelines among many senior war veterans and young students gathered here to

USS Hornet at bay / 港灣邊的大黃蜂號

commemorate this Day of Infamy, as President Franklin D Roosevelt called it, a question comes at once to my mind. "Why is it so difficult for Japan to apologize and show remorse to China and Korea, as well as to the other nations of Asia that suffered immense injury and sorrow during WWII? Damages that were incurred in the Japanese war of aggression. Yet here in America, they can humbly admit to their guilt in front of the American people."

Suddenly I have a moment of realization. Japan lost the War to America. Many Japanese, perhaps to this day,

Japanese Consul General / 日本總領事
Commemorating Pearl Harbor / 珍珠港紀念日
USS Hornet / 大黃蜂號

do not accept mentally and psychologically that they lost the war to the other countries. To their minds, China, Korea, the Southeast Asian nations, even the British in Burma, were just collateral successors in the war, hanging to the coat tails of America.

Some Japanese probably think that, had America not entered the War, the result might have been vastly different. Had Japan not struck Pearl Harbor, they might just have prolonged their military successes in annexing much of Asia under the Imperial flag. For Japan had hugely underestimated America's resolve and military prowess.

While most Japanese have since learned the lesson of war and became peace-loving, there are always those die-hard militarists. But if any of them should feel they could have won the War without America's intervention, they are hugely miscalculating once again. Look no further than the Vietnam War, when America pitched its far superior forces against a primitive guerilla army, and lost.

While touching on the subject of apology, an analogy is Japan's reluctance to provide one for the comfort ladies. One need look no further than the flood of Japanese adult comic and online pornography to understand the psyche of the Japanese man, submitting even their own to the world, though virtually. Why would they care for other women? A study of such mentally, even academically, is perhaps appropriate.

It is a lesson of which not only Japan should take notice. Any potential aggressor should take heed before attempting to subdue other nations by force, weaker though such nations may seem. The Vietnam War, in which the USS Hornet played an active role, is a perfect example. National resolve and perseverance can take down the mightiest, a modern-day David against Goliath.

History is not made by supposition of what could have happened, but by what did happen. And it would be the USS Hornet that played a crucial role in the subsequent turn of events, as the aircraft carrier became the launching pad of America's first retaliation strike to Japanese aggression.

On this same morning, I had left Captain Moon Chin's home in Hillsboro where I am staying and had driven across the San Mateo Bridge to the East Bay to visit the USS Hornet. On it, there is a short description of the role that Moon, now 104 years old, played in evacuating Jimmy Doolittle after the Raid of Tokyo. I wanted to have a look at that description. Moon had declined my invitation to come along, as he had visited the Hornet on several special occasions.

Going up the bridge connecting the pier to the aircraft carrier's hangar deck, I had proceeded to purchase a ticket for the visit. Just as I showed my ID to take advantage of a senior discount, the fellow at the reception said, "Today everyone can visit for free; it is Pearl Harbor Day". How fortuitous that I should chance upon visiting at such a memorable time.

I entered the hangar just as they opened at 10am when there were hardly any visitors. In another hour or so, people would be pouring in for the commemoration ceremony which I described above. Inside the lower deck were many naval airplanes and helicopters, mostly from the Korean and Vietnam War era.

There were also on display the Apollo space capsule and the all-chrome quarantine Airstream used for the astronauts of the Apollo 11 and 12 missions. Opposite the Airstream that once held Neil Armstrong, Buzz Aldrin and Michael Collins (famed for the first mission to the moon in 1969) was the Sea King helicopter that retrieved the astronauts after they landed back on earth, splashing into the ocean. On the side of the helicopter are emblems signifying the multiple times of retrieval of the space capsule. The USS Hornet played a key role in the entire recovery effort.

But my attention was focused on an earlier mission that defined the turning point of WWII. Just four months after the commissioning of the USS Hornet, it became the platform that launched America's first strike into the heart of Japan's homeland. The current USS Hornet (CV-12) I am visiting is the successor of the earlier aircraft carrier carrying the same name (CV-8), which sank during the Battle of Santa Cruz shortly after a year in service, or better to say a year in combat. In my collection of war-time magazine, it included some rare Japanese military journal of WWII with pictures of the sinking of the USS Hornet.

USS Hornet's maiden voyage in combat saw the legendary aviator Jimmy Doolittle and his squadron of 16 B-25 bombers on board. As to be expected, the bombers could barely take off with the short runway, and it would have been impossible to land back on the carrier. Even for launching the bombers, the air controller had to wait for the aircraft carrier to go on a dip with the wave to flag the plane to take off. The timing must be perfect to match with the upward surge of the flight deck such that the plane could leave with a skyward angle. These sixteen B-25s were destined to bomb several industrial and military targets before heading into China to land.

Sinking of the USS Hornet / 擊沉大黃蜂   End of CV-8 Hornet / 大黃蜂 CV-8 沉入海底

Japanese war magazine cover /
日本軍事雜誌封面

But due to early detection by several small Japanese picket boats, the launch was brought forward by over two hundred miles and ten hours to avoid Japanese naval and air interception. After the bombing raid, the bombers arrived on China's coast at night. All the airplanes ran out of fuel and were lost to crashes on land or at sea, including one that deviated to the Russian coast. Miraculously, most flyers and crew survived, either bailing out or walking out of their crashed airplanes.

This strike boosted the morale of the Americans and Allies alike, and forced the Japanese to redeploy their forces for defense of their homeland. President Roosevelt told the American public that the bombers flew from Shangri-La, the mythical city in James Hilton's novel Lost Horizon.

The strike triggered the Battle of Midway two months later, as the Japanese thought the aircraft carrier was an unlikely launching pad for bombers, and thus focused on the Pacific island nearest to Japan instead. That sea battle would become the turning point of the War in the Pacific. Four of Japan's carriers, which had struck Pearl Harbor just six months earlier, were sunk, together with much of its fleet.

On the USS Hornet today, there is a special section, right next to the entrance, with a display devoted to the Doolittle Raid of Tokyo. Though there is no real-size B-25 specimen on display, smaller models and many photographs of the history-making endeavor graced the exhibit. It is here that Moon Chin enters the picture, with a description of his aviation valor and the evacuation of Jimmy Doolittle out of China, later to be decorated and promoted from a Lieutenant Colonel to become a Brigadier General. A full-page Life Magazine advertisement of the time even reads "Do More for Doolittle," encouraging Americans to buy more War bonds.

My own interest in warplanes and warships began when I was in high school, as a member of the Aviation Club started by the Jesuit Father Cunningham. He, as well as Father McKenzie later, were successive chaplains for American servicemen on warships visiting Hong Kong for R&R in the 1960s.

The priests used to invite me on their launch yacht to visit aircraft carriers, like the Kitty Hawk and the Coral Sea, moored outside of Hong Kong harbor. I even got to dine at the sailor's mess/canteen. That inspired me with a life-long interest in aviation. Fr. Cunningham SJ was unfortunately a casualty later in 1972 on a Cathay Pacific flight from Bangkok to Hong Kong on which a bomb was planted by an airport policeman with a plot to receive insurance payout.

Back at Captain Moon Chin's home, I showed the centenarian pilot pictures I took on the flight deck of the USS Hornet. Posing next to an F-14 Tomcat, I had gestured for the fighter jet to take off. With that, Moon brought out from his cabinet an elegant box of Remy Martin Louis XIII brandy. He had saved it since the days when he owned and operated his civilian airline in Taiwan. Today, a bottle of that vintage would cost upward of $4000 USD.

I stopped Moon just in time from opening it, as I promised him that I would return again in the spring of 2018 and toast him on his 105th birthday, a perfect vintage for someone of vintage.

珍珠港

大黃蜂號航空母艦，美國對侵略者的第一個回應

「我們以最深的敬意與慰問，代表日本人民及日本政府向戰爭中殞落的生命致歉。」日本駐舊金山總領事山田淳（Jun Yamada）開場時如此說。山田是引言人介紹上台的第一位講者，台上立著一面巨大的美國國旗，這裡是大黃蜂號的停機棚。

今天不是一般的日子，是非常特別的一天。七十六年前的今天，日本皇軍偷襲珍珠港，重創美國的太平洋艦隊。而今大黃蜂號停泊在阿拉米達舊金山灣內的一個碼頭旁，開放給大眾參觀。

山田總領事面對台下聽眾進一步述說美日兩國和解的過程，並感謝美國在戰後對日本的援助。山田湊巧與指揮滿州七三一部隊的將軍同名，這支部隊在第二次世界大戰期間，利用人體進行生化武器實驗，惡名昭彰。

典禮現場來了不少老兵和年輕學生，大家齊聚一堂紀念這個羅斯福總統稱之為國恥的日子。我站在一旁聽著台上的致詞，心中頓時浮現一個疑問：「日本為何始終不願向中國、韓國及其它亞洲國家致歉、懺悔？這些國家在二戰期間因為日本侵略而承受極大的傷痛。但是在這裡，日本人卻能謙卑地向美國人民悔過。」

我突然意識到，二戰結束日本只是對美國投降。也因此至今許多日本人在心裡或精神上仍然不接受日本戰敗給其他的國家。在他們看來，中國、韓國、東南亞國家甚至是駐緬甸的英軍，都只是在這場戰爭中因為美國的關係而成為既得利益者。

有些日本人或許認為，假如美國沒有參戰的話結果可能大為不同。假若日本沒有襲擊珍珠港的話，或許日本皇軍就可以繼續擴大併吞亞洲。然而，日本卻嚴重低估了美國的決心和軍事實力。

儘管日後多數日本人學到了戰爭的教訓，崇尚和平，但仍不乏強硬的軍國主義者。若他們仍認為只要沒有美國的介入，日本就能獲勝，那他們又再次嚴重誤判情勢了。只要回顧越戰就好了，美國雖然派出優勢的軍隊與裝備陽春的越南游擊軍作戰，但是最終還是戰敗了。

既然談到道歉，就不得不談到日本始終不願向慰安婦認真致歉一事。從日本氾濫的成人漫畫和網路情色就能看出日本男性的心理，他們甚至能讓自己國家的女性獻身給全世界（雖然只是虛擬世界）。如何還能期待他們會在乎其他女性？當然，這方面或許仍需要從心理及學術的角度做進一步的研究。

這樣的教訓不僅日本應該銘記，也是任何試圖以武力侵犯國力較弱的侵略者應該記取的。大黃蜂號在越戰中的角色就是最好的例子。一個國家的決心與毅力足以扳倒最強大的敵人，越戰就是大衛對抗歌利亞的現代翻版。

歷史並非假設過去可能如何，而是記載確實發生過的事。大黃蜂號正是在後來情勢變化中扮演關鍵的角色，成為美國開始反擊日本侵略的跳板。

我住在機長陳文寬位於希爾斯伯勒的家，今天早晨，我從他家開車越過聖馬刁大橋，來到東灣參觀大黃蜂號。艦上有一段關於陳文寬的介紹，現在已經一百零四歲的他曾在東京大轟炸後協助杜立德將軍撤離。我想要親眼看一看這段記載。陳文寬並沒有應我的邀約一同前來，因為他早在許多特殊的場合參訪過大黃蜂號。

我走上連接碼頭和航母停機棚甲板的橋，準備買票入場。出示身分證想看看有沒有敬老折扣時，售票員卻說：「今天是珍珠港日，所有人都能免費入場。」我居然能在這麼值得紀念的日子到訪，真是太碰巧了。

早上十點展場門一開，我就進到停機棚，這時候還沒有什麼訪客。一個多小時後，人潮開始湧進我剛提過的紀念典禮現場。下層甲板展示許多海軍的飛機和直升機，大多來自韓戰及越戰時期。

展出的還有阿波羅號太空艙，及一輛全鉻材質的 *Airstream* 拖車，用來隔離出過阿波羅 11 號和 12 號任務的太空人。*Airstream* 的對面是海王直升機，曾載過阿姆斯壯、艾德林和柯林斯這些參與過一九六九年登月任務的知名太空人。太空人返回地球後降落在海上，海王直升機的任務則是負責由海上接回他們。機身側邊有象徵多次成功回收太空艙的標誌，顯示大黃蜂號在整個回收任務中扮演的關鍵角色。

但我最感興趣的，是更早期一個扭轉二戰情勢的任務。大黃蜂號服役後四個月，就成了美國第一波轟炸日本本土的跳板。我參觀的大黃蜂號（*CV-12*）是〈*CV-8*〉下一代的航母。

B-25 taking off / B-25 奔向天際　　Madame Chiang honoring Doolittle / 宋美齡女士表彰杜立德

CV-8 服役或應該說參戰屆滿一年後不久，便在聖克魯斯群島戰役中被擊沉。在我收藏的幾本珍貴二戰軍事雜誌中，就有幾張 CV-8 遭擊沉的罕見照片出自日軍日誌。

大黃蜂號首航任務搭載的正是傳奇飛行員吉米・杜立德和他的十六架 B-25 轟炸機中隊。這些轟炸機如同預料，根本無法在這麼短的跑道起飛，起飛後也無法再降落到航母。因此塔台更必須等到航空母艦隨著海浪下傾時，才能指示飛機預備起飛。時機必須分毫不差，須等到飛行甲板隨著海浪再上揚時，剛好讓飛機有足夠的角度起飛。這十六架 B-25 負責轟炸若干工業和軍事目標，隨後飛往中國降落。

然而，由於艦隊過早被幾艘日軍哨艇發現，逼得飛機必須提前十小時起飛，等於要多飛兩百英里以避開日本海空軍的攔截。執行轟炸任務後，隊伍於晚上飛抵中國海岸。燃料已經耗盡，不是墜毀在陸地就是墜入海中，還有一架甚至偏離航道飛到俄羅斯的海岸。奇蹟似的，大多數的飛官和機組人員透過跳傘或是自行逃出墜毀的機艙而倖存。

Display on USS Hornet / 大黃蜂號上的展出
USS Hornet kitchen / 艦上伙房

轟炸行動大大地提振美國和盟軍的士氣，迫使日軍重新佈署軍隊回防日本本土。羅斯福總統向美國人民說，這些轟炸機是從香格里拉起飛的，詹姆士・希爾頓《失落的地平線》中杜撰的人間天堂。

這場轟炸點燃了兩個月後的中途島海戰，日本判斷大黃蜂號應該沒有辦法讓轟炸機起飛，因此將重心放在最接近日本的太平洋島嶼。這場海戰成了太平洋戰爭的轉捩點。六個月前，偷襲珍珠港的四艘日本航空母艦及大部分艦隊均在此戰役被擊沉。

今天大黃蜂號的出口旁有一個杜立德空襲東京的特展。雖然沒有展出真的 B-25，但是有模型機和許多創造這段歷史的照片。這場特展裡也介紹了陳文寬，記載了他英勇的飛行事蹟，以及他協助杜立德撤離中國的經過，杜立德後來從中校晉升到旅長。《生活雜誌》當時還有一則寫著「 Do More for Doolittle 」〈為杜立德加油〉的全頁廣告，鼓勵美國人購買戰爭債券。

我從高中開始對戰機和戰艦產生興趣，還參加過耶穌會教士康寧漢神父發起的航空社。他與麥肯錫神父在一九六零年代陸續成為來香港休假，在美軍戰艦上的牧師。

兩位神父曾邀我搭他們的快艇去參觀停泊在香港港外的航空母艦,像是小鷹號和珊瑚海號。我甚至還在艦上的海軍食堂吃過飯。這樣的經歷啟發了我一生對飛航的興趣。康寧漢神父不幸在一九七二年的一場空難中去世,當時他搭上國泰航空從曼谷飛往香港的班機,有一名航警為了詐領保險金於是在機艙內裝了炸彈。

回到機長陳文寬的家,我拿出我在大黃蜂號甲板上拍的照片給百歲機長看。一張我自己在 F-14 雄貓式戰機旁擺出指示戰機起飛的姿勢。陳文寬隨即從櫃子裡拿出一瓶相當雅緻的人頭馬路易十三白蘭地。那瓶是他在台灣創辦民航事業時就一直珍藏的。如今這樣的陳年好酒一瓶可能要價四千美元以上。

我及時阻止他開瓶,我答應他,等二零一八年春天他一百零五歲生日時我會再回來敬他一杯,用一支好酒敬一位非凡的長者。

F-14 on flight deck /
HM 在飛行甲板上與 F-14 合影

探索欽敦江的上游

EXPORING
UPPER REACHES
OF THE
CHINDWIN RIVER

Khamti, Myanmar – January 20, 2018

EXPORING UPPER REACHES OF THE CHINDWIN RIVER

For the last two weeks, my team and I have been exploring the upper reaches of the Chindwin River, a major tributary of the Irrawaddy. The area is home to the Naga people, former headhunters inhabiting the border of Myanmar and India.

We met our exploration boat HM Explorer docked at Khamti on the middle Chindwin River, waiting for me and my team to fly in from Mandalay. Just slightly over three months ago, I reached the source of the Irrawaddy River in southeastern Tibet, and now we are on one of the most important tributaries of the same river. I have always wanted to explore the Chindwin and its upper reaches. So far, it has brought me to Khamti four times, each time making an effort to go a little further and find out more upriver.

Now we are sailing upstream rather than upriver, as the Chindwin becomes only navigable to small boats. We abandoned the comfort of our boat with seven cabins, electricity and a well-stocked bar, and moved on to tiny sampan-like wooden boats with long-tail motors. Each of these boats can barely fit three persons, with the waterline a few inches below us. In case the boat tips over, we all have our life vests on. However, should the boat flip, these life vests may not be adequate to save

HM Explorer as base / 我們的基地 HM Explorer

us, as many water snakes are seen in this section of the river, swimming with their heads showing above the water.

About an hour into a narrow gorge, perhaps some fifty meters wide, we reach a whitewater rapid. This was the end of our exploration three years ago. This time, I am determined to continue and advance further. We change into a yet smaller boat, each taking two passengers, and challenge the fast running drop of the river to reach some protruding rocks adjacent to the rapids. We disembark onto a narrow wooden plank to get our feet on the rock. Helpers carried our bags, including tents and sleeping bags. Drinking water, snacks such as power bars and cookies, and even beer, are important amenities for such excursions. The last item is particularly important for boosting our energy.

A quick hike up past a convenience store in a shed and then we descended some boulders. Three larger cargo boats were moored along the side. We boarded one, about ten meters in length, and the big diesel engine roared upstream with the eight of us. Fifteen minutes later, another rapid appeared in front. We again dismounted from the cargo *boat and hiked some more, this time above and around a small mound of rocks, and descended to take yet another boat that was smaller, but nonetheless could fit us all.*

Within a matter of two hours, we had switched boats in relay four times before reaching Taikti Village. Along the way, the many big and small gold mining operations along the river were both alarming and disheartening, especially for a naturalist like Dr. Bleisch, our Science Director in the team.

We are now at the border of Sagaing Division and Kachin State. A small army camp guards the beach where the boat dropped us off. A soldier with a semi-automatic rifle paced the riverbank to keep an eye over traffic passing, or trespassing. The Kachin Independence Army (KIA), an insurgent group that has existed in upper Myanmar for decades, are said to roam nearby. The group controls much of the hill country within Kachin State, from the Indian border all the way across to the Chinese side in Yunnan. The Myanmar government may have a tenuous hold on transportation and communication routes only.

Small boat upriver / 乘小船前往上游

Sandra, our young and capable Myanmar Country Manager, went ahead to negotiate with the Army for us to continue the river journey. She came back disappointed, as a special permit must be issued at Khamti. I reckon this will be the farthest north on the Chindwin we will reach, for now.

We are here during winter's low water season, but from markings on the riverbank trees, I can surmise that, during high water rainy season, the Chindwin will overflow the banks, and the entire beach will disappear. We proceed up the hill as the village is within a fifteen-minute walk from where we land.

We visit the village with one main street, stopping by two Naga bamboo houses. I see a motorcycle coming by carrying a camouflage-clothed militia man with machine guns on his back. The place seems always on the alert and militarized, even for some civilians. After an hour or so of roaming the village, we begin our journey back.

By now in the afternoon, river traffic has virtually stopped up and down river. We manage to hire a boat, but the owner is only willing to go part of the way. We stop for the night to camp out along one of the many sand banks.

Relaying upriver / 接力換船   Goldminer along river / 河邊淘金

Casual army / 悠閒的軍隊
Militia with gun / 揹著槍的民兵

The bonfire made from some gathered drift wood keeps the winter evening warm and cheerful.

Using the same fire, Zaw Phyoe Aung, our boat chef, and Wai Phyoe Thant, our boat captain, help warm up the pre-cooked food we brought along. In such a location and situation, simple fried rice tastes better than a full meal of multiple dishes on our boat. Even the junk food I brought along is junky no more.

The following morning, like every morning since we arrived in Myanmar, was very foggy and visibility was only ten meters or so. The sky usually would not clear up for a couple of hours after sunrise. Bill Bleisch, again like every morning, would roam the nearby forest to seek out birds from their songs. And here we were lucky to see a few Pied Hornbills gliding high above us, crossing the Chindwin River.

At many locations where we spent the night, Bill would set up camera traps and went to bed with the hope of retrieving photo images of some nocturnal animals in the forest the following morning. Though mostly disappointed, naturalists today must learn to live on hope, given the state of our modern world. Our young intern, Charlie, joining us during his gap year, provided some additional hope for the future.

Xavier documented as much as possible on film. Not only points of interest, but the record of our own activities may become important archival data someday, perhaps decades from now. Looking back at our earlier footage taken during expeditions some thirty years ago reveals much of value that is both historic and no longer exists, or even nostalgic.

At mid-morning, we hike to a nearby gold mine camp and negotiated a boat to continue our journey back downstream to our base boat, again going through the relay of four different types of boats, but in reverse order. Unlike some explorers today who are fixated on reaching a destination in one go, I have always been prepared to turn back when the situation prohibits further advances. Nonetheless I don't simply take "No" as an answer, and would instead push for a conditional "Yes". It seems to work time and again, though at times I would have to return after a long hiatus to secure a "Yes" to further my exploration.

So far, the uppermost Chindwin continues to evade my full exploration. For now, I have to satisfy myself by moving my fingers upstream on my iPad satellite image of the river, enlarging a whole region where jungle and river merges, with occasional plains where the river has left immense footprints of dozens, even scores of ox-bow lakes. Those look like perfect resting and wintering grounds for migrating birds from the Tibetan plateau to the north beyond the eastern Himalayas.

I know some day, hopefully soon, I will set my feet upon that beautiful landscape.

探索欽敦江的上游

過去兩週，我和團隊一同探索欽敦江的上游，這條江河是伊洛瓦底江主要的支流。那個區域是那迦人的故鄉，他們曾是獵頭族，居住在緬印邊境一帶。

我們一行人從曼德勒飛抵坎迪，與已經停泊在欽敦江中游等著我們的 *HM Explorer* 會合。就在三個多月前，我才抵達伊洛瓦底江位於西藏東南方的源頭，現在我們又來到這一條河最重要的支流上。我一直希望能夠探索欽敦江及這條河的上游地區所以至今已經四度造訪坎迪，每一次都試圖往上游再深入一點、多了解一點。

此刻我們逆流而上。這一段的欽敦江只能容納小型船，於是我們放棄了擁有七個空調座艙、供有電力及酒吧且備貨充足的探險船，轉搭似小型舢舨的木舟，木舟尾裝有馬達。每艘木舟勉強可以載三個人，吃水線離我們下方只有幾英寸。一夥人都穿上救生衣，以防翻船。不過，即便穿上這些救生衣，恐怕也救不了我們，這個河段都是水蛇，牠們游在水裡時還會把頭探出水面。

進到寬約五十公尺的峽谷約一小時後，我們碰上湍流。三年前我們正是在此止步的，但是這次我決定無論如何都要繼續挺進。我們再次改搭更小的船，每艘乘坐兩位乘客，準備勇渡眼前的湍流，抵達與湍流毗連的突出岩塊。我們靠著窄木板下了船，助手替我們

Taikti market / Taikti 的市場

Make-shift dining site / 簡易的用餐區
Riverbank camp / 在河灘紮營
A Naga home / 那迦人的家

扛著裝有帳篷和睡袋的行李。飲用水、高熱量棒、餅乾甚至啤酒都是這趟跋涉中不可或缺的物品，尤其是啤酒，有助提振我們的精神。

我們往上走一小段路後經過一家用棚子搭起的雜貨店，接著走下幾顆巨石。三艘大貨船就停泊在一旁。我們登上其中一艘，船身十公尺，柴油引擎轟隆隆載著我們八人繼續逆流向上。十五分鐘後，再次遇上湍流。我們再度下船爬了一小段路，上上下下一堆岩石塊，再換搭另一艘更小但是足以容納我們八人的船。

我們在短短兩小時內接連換了四次船才抵達了 Taikti 村。一路上看見沿岸大大小小開採中的金礦，實在令人憂愁心痛，尤其對我們團隊的自然學家兼科學主任畢蔚林博士來說。

抵達了實皆省和克欽邦的邊境，一下船便看見駐守河岸的小軍營，一名手持半自動步槍的士兵沿著河岸監控所有人車或擅闖者。據說，克欽獨立軍會在附近出沒，這支叛軍已在北緬甸活動幾十年。

他們控制了克欽邦內大部分的山區，一路橫跨印度邊境至中國雲南。緬甸政府對於該地的交通和通訊管道沒什麼實質的控制權。

我們能幹的緬甸經理珊卓，前去與當地政府協商，好讓我們能夠繼續探河之行。但是她沮喪地回來，因為必須得取得在坎迪發行的特別通行證才能通關。我估計這次北溯欽敦江只能在此打住。

此行適逢枯水期，但是從河岸樹木的水痕我可以推測，汛期欽敦江會淹上河岸，淹沒整片河灘。從下船處往山上步行十五分鐘才能抵達村落。

我們走訪了這個只有一條主要道路的村落，經過兩間那迦人的竹屋。這時我看到一台摩托車過來，上面載著一個身著迷彩、揹著機槍的民兵。這裡似乎隨時都維持高度警戒與武裝的狀態，甚至連平民也是。在村裡逛了一個鐘頭左右，我們開始往回走。

現在已經是下午了，往上下游的船基本上都不開了。我們還是想辦法弄到一艘船，但是船夫只願意載我們一小段路。我們只好找了一處河灘紮營過夜，撿拾漂流木生起營火讓冬天的夜晚多了份溫暖和喜悅。

隨船廚師 *Zaw Phyoe Aung* 和船長 *Wai Phyoe Thant* 替我們把帶來的熟食放到營火上加熱。在這樣的環境下，簡單的炒飯遠遠勝過探險船上的全餐。連我攜帶的垃圾食物都不再是垃圾食物了。

翌日早晨起了濃霧，能見度約僅十公尺，我們抵達緬甸後的每天早晨都是如此。天空要等到日出後兩個小時才會晴朗開來。畢蔚林博士每天早上的例行公事，就是到附近樹林靠著鳥鳴以尋覓它們的蹤跡。我們很幸運看見幾隻冠斑犀鳥從我們的上空飛過，穿越欽敦江。

夜宿河灘的時候，畢蔚林博士在入睡前會先在附近設下相機陷阱，希望能拍到森林中的夜行動物。雖然通常都拍不到東西，但是身處在現代世界的自然學家必須學著懷抱希望。我們年輕的實習生查理利用空檔的一年加入我們，從他身上我們看見未來又多了一份希望。

一路上李伯達盡可能攝影紀錄一切。不只是紀錄這趟的重點而已，還有團隊一路上種種的活動，這些在未來的一天有可能成為重要的檔案，那一天有可能是幾十年後的事。回顧三十幾年前我們拍攝的探險影片，在歷史上具有意義，當中有些人和事物現在已經消失了，非常令人懷念。

上午十點多，我們來到附近一處金礦場，雇到了一艘船，於是我們繼續往下游前進好跟在基地的船會合。跟來時一樣，我們換了四次不同的船，但順序與出發時是相反的。有些探險家堅持一次就要抵達目的地，而我不同，一旦情況不允許繼續前進的時候，我隨時都做好回頭的準備。但是我不會輕易地接受「不」這個答案，我會去爭取一個有條件的「可以」。這招還滿管用的，但是有些時候我必須停下來，為了可以確定未來我的探險是順利的。

至今，我還沒能如願一探欽敦江的最上游，所以只好打開我的 iPad 衛星圖往欽敦江上游滑，來滿足自己。我將某一處河流與叢林的匯聚處放大，出現了幾個平原，以及為數眾多的牛軛湖，那是欽敦江走過留下的巨大足跡。對那些從青藏高原到喜馬拉雅山脈東北側的候鳥而言，這裡可是休憩和過冬的絕佳地點。

我知道有一天，希望是不久的將來，我又會踏上這塊美麗的土地。

Taikti shop owner / Taikti 的商店老闆

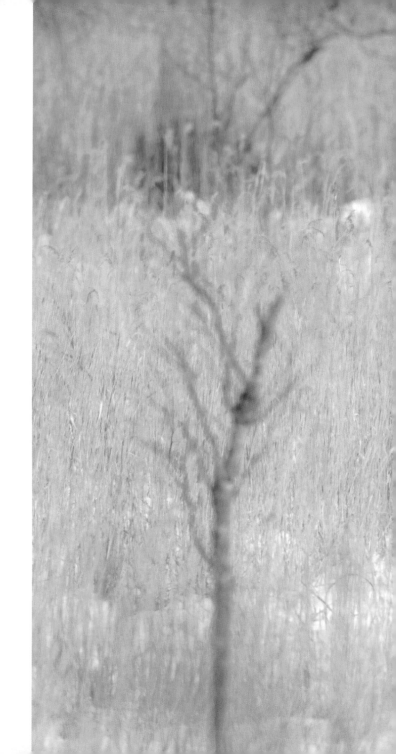

我
對
野
生
動
物
攝
影
的
看
法

MY TAKE ON
WILDLIFE
PHOTOGRAPHY

Kushiro, Japan – February 10, 2018

MY TAKE ON WILDLIFE PHOTOGRAPHY
Winter in Hokkaido

Winter in eastern Hokkaido sees not only a convergence of migrating birds, but also one of the largest concentrations of active cameras, lenses and tripods. At locations where the Red-crowned Cranes are regularly roosting or feeding, photographers flock from all over Japan, and now also from around the world.

The recent arrival of photographers from China, professionals or aspiring pros, further crowded the few locations where the cranes are known to be active during the day. Scheduled artificial feeding draws the cranes to these locations. These sites now resemble the Olympic press box circle... or circus! This being winter, it's the Winter Olympics, as we are surrounded everywhere by snow.

Since my first rendezvous with the Red-crowned Crane and the sea eagles many years ago, I have tried to return every winter, not unlike a ritual pilgrimage to a religious site. In the beginning, I brought along my largest lens and tripod, just like everyone else. Two Nikons, a 600mm and a 300mm fast lens in rare white coating, with 1.4 and 2X extension converters.

Soon I realized there was no need to use such heavy and apprehension-inducing devices. Let alone my ageing arm would soon become aching arm. There was no need even to impress others, an act which some serious amateurs as well as novices occasionally try to do. Every photographer was armed with an arsenal of big 'weapons', mostly with camouflage cover. Whether that was to insulate the equipment against the extreme weather or to pretend to blend into a treeless environment at fixed shooting locations was beyond my comprehension.

These heavy cameras and lenses are only a liability, limiting the agile movement called for in such photography. It is not an asset at all. The tripod is even more of a hindrance, prohibiting easy and fast maneuvering to follow a bird in flight. The only use of a tripod is for steadying the heavy devices when shooting the birds on the ground. In such cases, a pivotal monopod just to help carry the weight may serve better. For me, I generally rest my camera on the tall fence for support.

Today, with digital cameras that allow for ISO settings upward of 6400, thus giving speed settings into the thousandth of a second complementing a lower f-stop to provide more depth of field, there is no question of capturing a moving object like a bird, and no need to worry about unstable hands of a photographer affecting the results due to motion. Such advances in cameras have rendered the use of a tripod a liability, especially in its limitation of fast movement of the camera to follow a moving target. Think of a marksman with a

Winter 2017 / 二零一七年冬季
HM without tripod / 不帶三腳架的 HM
Winter 2012 / 二零一二年冬季

skeet rifle using a tripod and one would get the point I'm trying to make.

Of course, if a photographer is still bent on photographing the grace of the crane on the ground, their courtship dance and other activities, perhaps having a tripod is still called for. But such photographs can soon become mundane and redundant, bordering on boring, and never quite enough of a challenge for a seasoned photographer. For me, the greatest satisfaction is to capture the birds in flight or a composition on a frame with specific crane or cranes.

Climate, especially drastic climate like during a snowstorm, provides for that climactic moment. I have always believed that drastic weather provides for the most dramatic pictures. Full sunshine is counter productive to the discriminating photographer, unless the shadow-play provides for some measured opportunities.

For photographing wildlife, I've always found the use of fixed focal length more conducive than having a zoom lens. The singular length allows me to focus on the subject matter, and not be distracted by more options and possibilities. For me, that is more important than having variable choices of focal length. My choice has been a 300mm f2.8 lens for the job, occasionally with a 2X converter. Others may dispute the quality of a 2X, but my failing eyesight, counting down to 70 years old, make such issues irrelevant.

While on the subject of sharp focus and clarity, let me define my own philosophy on this matter in photography. There are pictures for which I pursue extreme sharp focus, especially when dealing

Owl / 貓頭鷹   Eagle in flight / 翱翔的海鷹

with scientific subjects, like aerial photos for geographic study, insects using micro or macro lenses, features of architecture, even portraits illustrating specific elements of character. But when I am photographing a scenic subject or even a moving object, at times clarity is not what I seek, but the mood or motion.

Therefore, seeking sharpness and clarity is not absolute, and at times counter-productive. To be obsessed with such a pursuit, especially for those with more advancing age, can be compared to a person with failing ears going out for the best music speaker with high fidelity that only an electronic instrument can detect, whereas their own physical faculties can no longer discern.

My long study and observation of the crane, in particular the Black-necked Crane of Tibet since 1988, has allowed me to understand their every gesture and movement. Certain calls can signify readying for flight, together with a straightened neck at a fixed angle tilting in a forward pos-

Eagle catching or missing prey / 海鷹捕捉獵物或沒有抓到的一刻   Fox / 狐狸

ture. Running starts for flight and wing motion for landing are guided by certain routines of wings and body.

As with the Sea Eagles, both the White-tailed and the Steller's species, they are guided by another set of rules which would manifest themselves to the beholder after extended observations. I find it most challenging not when the eagle is in flight, at rest, or even grabbing a fish with its talons; it is most gratifying to catch one of these majestic birds in flight making a fast turn to descend on its prey. It may not be the most graceful shot, but it is something which reflects the instantaneous decision and motion of the bird.

By the way, as reference, I use spot focus on such outings, with a hit rate of 2 to 1 in terms of focus and capturing the object within the frame. In other words, I may delete 1 out of 3 pictures I shoot. This may be superfluous compared to many photographers by my side who fire off their shutters like a machine gun, then spend time deleting most of the pictures of the shoot.

Another note of interest, perhaps due in part to my own stubbornness, since my early days of photography, including during my several years stint at the National Geographic, I have always treated my shutter with respect, considering it sacred and pushing it to take shots, one at a time. This is perhaps a remnant from before, when film was treated as a rare and limited commodity.

Though I have had a motor-drive attached to all my cameras since my first Nikon FTN of 1974 era,

Crane in flight / 空中的鶴

I have never, not once, fired off my shutter with a motor. I have only used it as a simple film winder. The current digitizing of all my slides images since 1974 can verify to that effect. In fact, my philosophy and mentality from the film era has not abated to this day. For me, digital photography with large memory capacity does not mean unlimited resources at hand. A disciplined use of the camera with respect would yield results of due value.

HM with camera / HM 與照相機

Yes, some perfect shots require a bit of luck, and I must confess to having a few of those very special moments. I am not one who would stand in the snow waiting for things to happen. In fact, I don't even have the patience to wait out a sunrise or a sunset. But snow scene and shadow often play a wonderful backdrop as a stage made by nature, where the wildlife, be it a crane, a swan, a goose, an owl, an eagle, a deer or a fox, can be the main actor or supporting actors.

With that in mind, I am always ready to lug my simple equipment and, with a cheery mood, dressed up warmly, head out into the cold snow-bound winter wilderness of Hokkaido. For now, I have my reservation at my favorite farmhouse abode again for next winter, right adjacent to one of the perfect sites where the crane return everyday during the winter.

我對野生動物攝影的看法　北海道的冬天

冬季的北海道東部不僅候鳥群聚，更是相機、鏡頭和三腳架最密集的地方之一。只要是丹頂鶴時常棲息覓食的地方，都會吸引大批來自日本甚至是世界各地的攝影師。

這幾年，來自中國的專業或想成為專業攝影師的人也大批湧進丹頂鶴會出沒的幾個地方。這幾個地點因為會在固定時候餵食，吸引鶴群前來。這些地方就好似奧運的媒體採訪區，也有點像馬戲團。由於正值寒冬，身處冰天雪地，或許說是冬奧會更貼切。

多年前遇見丹頂鶴和海鷹後，每年冬天猶如朝聖一般，我都會設法回來這裡。一開始，我和其他人一樣，會帶最大的鏡頭、三腳架，兩台 Nikon，以及少見的白色鍍膜 600 毫米和 300 毫米快速鏡頭，再配上 1.4 倍及 2 倍的增倍鏡。

但是我很快地發覺根本用不著這些笨重又令人不心安的裝備，更何況我逐漸退化的手臂可能很快地會痠痛起來。實在也沒必要去炫耀裝備，但是一些認真的業餘攝影師和新手有時還是會克制不住。每個人都配帶強大的「軍火」，大多都有偽裝罩。不管是為了在寒冬下替裝備保暖，或是為了在定點拍攝時融入一棵樹都沒有的環境裡，種種行徑都令我難以理解。

這些笨重的相機和鏡頭只是累贅，讓攝影師在這種需要動作靈活拍攝的環境下綁手綁腳，一點幫助也沒有。三腳架更是礙事，無法讓攝影師可以快速地跟上正在飛的鳥。只有在拍停留地面的鳥時，三腳架才能發揮穩定這些裝備的作用。這種時候，使用剛好能支撐相機重量的單腳架效果會更好。而我，通常會將相機放在有一定高度的圍籬上作為支撐。

現在的數位相機感光度都可上調至 6400 或以上，快門速度可快達千分之一秒，彌補了低光圈值的不足，拍攝出來的畫面更具景深，要拍到飛鳥等移動中的物體，根本不是問題，也不必擔心手震影響拍攝品質。相機技術這麼進步，使用三腳架就顯得累贅，尤其限制了攝影師迅速跟拍移動目標的能力。只要試想神槍手拿著裝上三腳架的步槍射擊飛靶，就會明白我的意思。

當然，假使攝影師仍希望拍出鶴在地面上的優雅姿態，捕捉牠們的求偶舞和其他動作的畫面，或許還是用得上三腳架。但是拍出來的照片可能就很一般甚至無趣，對老練的攝影師來說一點挑戰性都沒有。對我來說，最大的成就感是拍攝在飛的鶴，或是畫面中呈現出一隻鶴或多隻鶴的構圖。

天候，尤其像暴風雪這樣激烈的氣候給了難得的片刻。我始終認為，在極端的天候下拍出來的照片是最有張力的。對挑剔的攝影師而言，除非恰好有陰影適合拍攝，否則出大太陽反而拍不出好照片。

拍攝野生動物時，我一直覺得鏡頭用固定焦距比變焦更好。單一鏡距讓我能聚焦在目標物上，而不受其他選項和可能性的影響。對我來說這比起可選擇多種鏡頭焦距來得更重要。我會帶上一個 300 毫米、f2.8 級的鏡頭，偶爾會帶 2 倍的增倍鏡。或許有人質疑 2 倍鏡的拍攝品質，但是年近七十的我，視力越來越差，這種問題就顯得不是那麼重要了。

既然談到拍攝的銳利度和清晰度，就不得不談我自己的看法。有些照片我會要求極銳利的對焦，尤其是跟科學有關的時候，像是地理研究的空拍圖、需透過顯微鏡頭或微距鏡頭拍攝的昆蟲照、建築物的特寫，甚至是必需表現出特定風格特徵的人物照。但是拍風景照或移動中物體時，我追求的不是清晰度，而是一種情境或動態。

所以說追求銳利度和清晰度並非是絕對的，有時反而適得其反。特別是慢慢有了年紀的人，太過執著於清晰與銳利，就如同聽力越來越差的人，卻要求高保真度的頂級音響，那種保真度可能只有電子儀器才測得出來，他們的聽力早已經無法分辨了。

從一九八八年開始我長期研究、觀察鶴，特別是西藏的黑頸鶴，從中讓我了解到牠們每個姿勢和動作。一些叫聲可能代表準備起飛，牠們會伸直脖子，以某個固定的角度前傾。助跑起飛和降落時翅膀及身體動作也有固定的模式。

海鷹則完全不同，白尾海鷹和虎頭海鷹也是，只要觀察一段時間就能看得出來。我發現，最大的挑戰並不是拍到飛行中、靜態的或伸出利爪抓魚的海鷹；而是捕捉到牠們急轉俯衝捕捉獵物的畫面才是最令我滿意的。或許這樣的畫面並不是最優雅的，但是卻能看出海鷹在瞬間所做的判斷和動作。

此外，我習慣使用點對焦拍攝海鷹，就對焦及讓目標物入鏡來說，命中率為二比一，也就是我每拍三張照片就會刪去一張。但是對我身旁眾多的攝影師來說，這動作也許顯得多餘，他們按快門的速度像機關槍般，拍完後再花時間把大部分的照片刪除。

還值得一提的是，從早期開始攝影，包括我在美國《國家地理雜誌》服務的那幾年，我對快門始終抱持著敬畏的態度，認為快門是神聖的，所以我堅持一張照片按一下快門。這或許和我固執的個性有關，也或許是經歷過早期底片尚屬珍貴的年代，而留下來的習慣吧。

儘管從我第一台一九七四年 Nikon FTN 開始，後來所有的相機都裝了捲片馬達，但我從沒有搭配快門使用過，只作單純的當捲片器使用。我從一九七四年以來拍的膠片正在數位化，這些影像正可以證明。至今，我仍抱持著早期底片時代我對於攝影的理念和心態。對我來說，即便已進入數位攝影的時代，相機容量龐大，並不代表資源用之不盡。唯有懷著誠敬的心，謹慎地使用手中的相機，才能創造出具有真正有價值的影像。

要拍到完美的照片的確需要點運氣。坦白說，我曾經碰過幾次這樣的天時地利人和。我不是那種會站在雪地裡等待時機降臨的攝影師，實際上我也沒有那種等看日出或日落的耐心。然而，雪景和陰影確實提供了絕妙的背景，在這個大自然搭起的舞台上，所有的野生動物都可以是主角，或是配角，不論是鶴、天鵝、雁、貓頭鷹、老鷹、鹿或狐狸。

抱著這樣的態度，我隨時可以帶上精簡的裝備，抱著雀躍的心情，穿上保暖的衣服，擁抱北海道冰封的野外冬景。為了明年冬天，我已經訂好了我最喜歡的農舍民宿，地點正好鄰近冬季鶴群天天會返回群聚的地方。

我
的
東
京
探
險

MY
TOKYO ESCAPADE

Tokyo – February 14, 2018

MY TOKYO ESCAPADE

The sushi bar had just handed out the last number for guests waiting outside. Turning around, we chose Robata, a corner restaurant down the street, just two blocks from the subway station at Shinbashi. The sign read something about "Hokkaido" cuisine, a place close to my heart where I just came from, after spending my annual ritual with the cranes and sea eagles. Outside, there is a waterwheel spinning.

Robata turned out to be a place specializing in hotpot and barbeque dishes, but perhaps only known to local Japanese customers. Ro-ba-ta - the three characters meant "pot cook in front." Just so, guests sat around a stage where a covered pot with multiple sections stood. Inside were a variety of cooked foods in a soup base.

We chose to sit at a table by the window. Our friend Saito helped with ordering, both the hotpot and the meat and seafood on sticks, grilled. Most tables were taken up, with a few younger diners sitting around the stage. The hotpot environment offered additional warmth for anyone coming in from the cold air outside. Soon our food began arriving, and I savored it with a cup of warm sake wine. As our table was right next to the door, each time someone came in, my back could feel the freezing air, as this was only mid February.

At around 7:30 pm, a middle-aged gentleman in traditional Japanese attire came through the cloth screen curtain from the kitchen behind. He proceeded to climb on stage where the pot had been covered and pushed forward to make space. The gentleman had on an orange-crimson costume. He knelt down on a small cushion, took out a small folded fan in one hand and a small handkerchief in the other. Then he took off the crimson outer jacket and was now left with the orange buttoned shirt, loose and tied to one side at an angle.

He began telling what seemed like a few light jokes as the audience stopped eating and listened intently while laughing occasionally. Then the more serious storytelling began. Despite not knowing any Japanese, I could tell from his gestures, facial expression, voice alternation and hand motions, that he was impersonating several characters at the same time.

The storytelling lasted half an hour during which the dining seemed to have come to a stall as everyone was watching and listening intently. The story must have been very captivating from the concentration I could see among the beholders. A sign with a handwritten paper tablet hung to the side of the stage. Written with heavy ink brush strokes, it designated today's show title.

Robata restaurant / 爐端燒餐廳
Hot pot cooked on stage / 檯前的關東煮
Diners around stage / 客人圍檯而坐

On the right side of the title was written today's date, on the left was written that this is the five thousand one hundred and eighty-ninth episode.

Saito explained to me that such acts are called Rakugo. It has a very long history and tradition, though today it has totally disappeared except in a few very specialized performance theaters. To find such a performance at a place like a restaurant is almost unheard of. The lady owner of this restaurant must be a fan herself, in order to provide the space and time for the act to be performed, interrupting the ordering and serving of food and dining.

As I left the restaurant, I really felt like coming back to see the next show. But the performance happens only every other day. I did come back two nights later, myself sitting next to the stage so as to be closer to the act. Surprisingly, the evening staged a different artist, a much younger fellow, performing the 5190th episode. He seemed to be more of a joke teller as his act drew a lot of laughter, with the young ladies in the audience all giggling away.

I have enjoyed drama since a young age. In high school I took small parts in Gilbert & Sullivan operettas, after high school I took the lead role in pre-collegiate stage dramas, and in college I acted in the Three Penny Opera and then even as a prince in a children's play, "Land of the Dragon". This storyteller artist seated in the center of diners brought back many fond memories of acting.

Despite this surprise discovery of Rakugo, Tokyo seems mundane and of little interest except for those bent on shopping and feasting. My own favorite has always been *Tokyu Hands*, the one in Shibuya that takes up seven main floors and twice as many sub-floors. It is not unusual that I would spend half a day plus a meal there, arriving at 10 am as the shop opens, and going home with an overload in bags of merchandise and gadgets, mostly cute gifts.

Opposite Tokyu Hands is another of my favorite stores which can easily take up another hour or two. *Montbell* has the best on offer in Japan for outdoor equipment. While my explorer's footprint may be found in Paragon at Union Square New York, Patagonia in Palo Alto, The North Face in San Francisco, and the multiple stores at Covent Garden in London, the Montbell store in Tokyo has much better fittings for an Asian sized person, let alone that Japanese are famous for gadgets, including outdoor ones. More shopping bags to come home with me.

I used to stay at the *Excel Hotel* right above the subway and train station in Shibuya. This gave me easy access to Tokyu Hands and the Montbell stores. The other attraction was looking down on the crosswalk, a real crosswalk, when the green light for pedestrians means crossing at all sides and crossing in the middle as well, a most spectacular sight. This is where a lot of tourists come to pay respect to the statue of the lone Japanese dog, sitting waiting

Rakugo young storyteller / 年輕的落語説書人
Expressive drama / 表演戲劇的張力

perpetually for the return of his master who never shows up. It was made into a movie starring Richard Gere.

But today home is not this well-placed hotel, but a real home in a residential high-rise building, courtesy of a close friend and CERS director. Suffice to say the rooms and balcony on the 42rd floor look out on the changing lights of the Tokyo Tower and the city panorama of Tokyo beyond. By day, the view was grand, and by night spectacular. It was also while staying at this home that I had the adventure exploring the restaurant in nearby Shinbashi with the Rakugo performing act.

There is another enclave, which most visitors to Tokyo may not know about, due to its small and hidden location in a back street of Takeshita where many tourists go shopping for trinkets. The Owl Village is a misnomer, as it is not a village, but an upstairs café that perhaps can fit at most eight guests at any one time. Thus it is important that reservations are made ahead of time.

Café is however the correct term as it serves only tea and coffee, nothing else. After all, guests come not even for the beverages which are a side show of low priority. They come to enjoy the company of a few species of owl kept in a small enclosed balcony. The owner/keeper would allow guests to put on a thick leather glove on one arm before proceeding to let an owl - even an eagle owl - to perch on the arm.

A beginner crash course is of course necessary before guests are allowed to handle these owls, some of which are famous for their unpredictable temperament. I was most fascinated to look at the colorful plume feather patterns of the various types of owls, a creation by nature that no high fashion designer can surpass.

My last stop, early in the morning before sunrise, is Tsukiji fish market. These are among the last days of the largest fish market in the world, as it will soon be moved to a new location, making way for the Olympics in another two years' time.

With Saito's help, he being a fish merchant, we were able to get special passes and observe the live tuna auction, which is now prohibited to tourists. The sing-song auctioneer performance with dramatic motion reminded me of the storyteller at the Robata restaurant, which also served up grilled tuna as one of its signature dishes. It all seems a good finale to my visit to Tokyo.

Owl Cafe specimens / 貓頭鷹咖啡館的珍寵
HM with Eagle Owl / HM 與鵰鴞

Tokyo by night / 東京夜景

我的東京探險

壽司吧收了最後一批在外頭排隊的客人，我們只好回頭，選了街角一家爐端燒餐廳，距離新橋地鐵站只有兩個路口。店家招牌寫著「北海道」料理，一個我喜愛的地方，我才剛從那裏結束每年拍攝丹頂鶴與海鷹的固定行程來到東京。這家店門口還有一台水車轉動著。

原來爐端燒專賣的是關東煮和燒烤，但是恐怕只有當地的日本客人才會知道。爐端燒這三個字的意思是「爐子放在前面烹煮」。客人圍坐在檯前，檯內擺著一鍋關東煮，格子內放著各種用高湯烹煮的食材。

我們選了窗邊的位置，好友 Saito 幫我們點餐，有關東煮、肉和海鮮的燒烤串。店裡的桌子大多都坐滿了，爐前坐了幾個年輕客人。熱熱的關東煮讓寒風中進門的客人感受溫暖。菜很快地陸續上桌，我配著溫清酒，一道道品嚐。我們因為坐在門邊，只要一有客人進門，我的背就會感到一股寒風，此時才二月中。

到了晚上七點半左右，一位身穿傳統日本服飾的中年紳士，從廚房布簾後走了出來。為了讓他爬上檯前，於是關東煮被蓋上並往前挪動，好騰出空間。這位紳士一身暗橘紅色，跪坐在小墊子上，一手拿著摺扇，另一手拿著手帕。他隨後脫掉暗橘紅色的外衣，裡面是一件扣子襯衫，鬆開的襯衫，把領帶撇到一邊。

他開始說起話來，應該是講了幾個笑話，因為客人放下了餐具仔細聽著，偶爾還會有些笑聲，但隨後便開始進入正題。儘管我完全不懂日語，但還是可以從他的姿勢、表情、聲音的變化和手勢，看得出來他一人分飾多角。

故事說了半小時，過程中，大家幾乎都放下碗筷，全神貫注地觀賞。從觀眾專注的眼神看來，講的故事肯定相當精彩。檯子旁掛著一個手寫的紙板，上面用墨黑毛筆寫著今天演出的主題，主題右側是當天日期，左側則寫著這是第 5189 回。

Saito 跟我說，這種表演稱作落語，有著悠久的歷史與傳統，但是如今，除了在少數幾個專門演出的劇場外，在外面已經看不到了。在餐廳看到這樣的演出幾乎是前所未聞。老闆娘肯定是個落語迷，才有辦法騰出空間和時間，在中斷點餐、上菜和用餐的情況下安排這樣的表演吧！

走出餐廳時，我真的很想要再回來看下一場表演。但是並不是天天都有表演，每隔一天才有。兩天後我又來光顧，挑了個舞台旁能近距離欣賞的位置。意外的是，那天晚上是一位年輕許多的落語家，演出第 5190 回。他似乎更會說笑，逗得客人哄堂大笑，連一旁的年輕小姐都咯咯笑著。

我從很年輕的時候就很喜歡戲劇。高中時演過吉伯特與沙利文喜劇類歌劇中的配角，進大學前演過舞台劇主角，大學時則演過《三便士歌劇》，之後甚至在兒童劇《Land of the Dragon》中飾演王子。這位端坐在客人中間的說書人讓我想起以前許多舞台上美好的記憶。

Tsukiji fish market / 築地魚市
Live auction of tuna / 鮪魚拍賣實況

雖然這次意外地發現了落語表演，但若非為了購物和美食而來，東京似乎沒什麼驚喜可言。我自己最愛的還是澀谷的那間東急手創館，共有七個主要的樓層和十四個次樓層。通常我會在這待上半天，早上十點營業時進來，在這吃一頓飯，然後回家時手上大包小包的各種玩意，大多是可愛的禮品。

東急手創館對面是另一家我也很喜歡的店，一進去就是一兩個鐘頭。Montbell 賣的是日本最棒的戶外裝備。身為探險家的我，足跡或許已經踏遍紐約聯合廣場的 Paragon、帕羅奧圖的 Patagonia、舊金山的 The North Face 及倫敦柯芬花園的幾家店，但是東京 Montbell 賣的尺寸還是比較適合亞洲人的身材，更別說日本以工具著稱，這當然也包括戶外裝備。逛完 Montbell 後，一袋袋都要跟我回家。

以往來到東京，我都會入住澀谷地鐵及火車站上面的卓越大飯店，因為很快就能到東急手創館和 Montbell。另一個吸引我的地方就是從樓上觀看下面的行人穿越道，是真正的行人穿越道，行人專用的綠燈亮起後，人潮開始從四周及中間穿越馬路，令人嘆為觀止。許多遊客也會來這裡向一座狗的雕像致敬，這隻狗一直坐在那裏等主人回來，但是主人卻沒有現身。這個故事後來還拍成了電影，李察・基爾主演。

但是這次來到東京住的地方不是這個交通方便的飯店，而是在一棟高樓大廈的住家，那是我的好友同時也是 CERS 董事的家。簡單來說，從四十二樓的房間和陽台向外一看，就能看到變換燈光的東京鐵塔，整個東京市景盡收眼簾。白天風景壯闊，晚上夜景動人。也因為住在這戶人家我才會在新橋附近找餐廳，遇見落語表演。

另一個秘境地方小，又隱藏在竹下通的巷子裡，因此，多數到東京的訪客可能都不知道有這樣的一個地方。許多遊客都會到竹下通購買小飾品。「貓頭鷹村」（The Owl Village）是大家對它的誤稱，因為這裡不是村落，而是一間在樓上的咖啡廳。由於任何時段店裡最多只能容納八個客人，要來最好提前訂位。

「咖啡廳」才是正確的用詞，因為店裡真的只賣茶和咖啡，沒有其他的東西。畢竟來這裡的客人不來喝飲料的。他們來這裡是為了可以享受跟幾種貓頭鷹在一個小小的封閉陽台上相處。老闆還是員工會讓客人先在一隻手戴上厚皮手套，才放貓頭鷹甚至是鵰鴞出來，停在客人的手上。

有一些貓頭鷹的脾氣是出了名的難以預測，所以客人必須聽完初學講習後，才能和貓頭鷹互動。各種貓頭鷹身上鮮豔的羽毛和圖樣非常吸引我，大自然的傑作，沒有高級時尚設計師可以媲美。

東京行的最後一站來到了築地魚市場，天都還沒亮。這次剛好碰上這個全球最大魚市營業的最後日子，因為不久後，這裡將成為兩年後東京奧運的預定地，魚市也將隨之遷至他處。

由於 Saito 恰好也是魚販，透過他的協助才有幸拿到特別通行證，能一睹鮪魚拍賣的現場實況，否則遊客是禁止入場的。拍賣人喊賣聲抑揚如曲，配上誇張的動作，讓我想起了爐端燒餐廳的說書人，而烤鮪魚是那裏的招牌菜之一。築地行成了我東京之旅的完美休止符。

杭
州
，
今
昔
四
十
載

HANGZHOU, FORTY YEARS AGO AND NOW

Hangzhou – March 25, 2018

HANGZHOU, FORTY YEARS AGO AND NOW

Growing up, I disdained reading stories with sad or tragic endings. So, I formed the habit of reading the last chapter of a book first. If a happy ending was not assured, I would not commit my time to reading the front part, thus saving myself time, emotion, and a few tears.

But today, I cry even reading a comic. Every book I read is like a sad story, bringing tears to my eyes. With any reading that extends beyond twenty minutes or so, my eyes automatically start watering, an annoying byproduct of ageing, at least in my case.

So, it is with such strained eyes that I review photographs I took in 1977 in Hangzhou, now stored as low-resolution images in my computer. But this time, tears came to my eyes both from age, as well from my sweet and beautiful memories being abruptly taken away.

I have taken over a quarter million photographs in China since first visiting the country in 1974. The only time I would recall those nostalgic images would be when I revisited a place and wanted to compare the then and the now. So here I am, from a budding explorer to a seasoned one, revisiting Hangzhou after forty years of absence.

As the Chinese saying goes, "Above there is heaven, below there are Suzhou and Hangzhou," a parody about the beauty and serenity of the two cities of coastal China. So, it is quite appropriate that, from the northern capital of Beijing, Qianlong, the most powerful and literarily sophisticated emperor of the Qing Dynasty, made six tours south of the Yangtze, each time stopping off at Hangzhou for extended stay.

Thanks to the courtesy of a dear friend Betsy of New York, who was celebrating her 75th birthday with relatives and close friends, I stayed at the posh Amanfayun Resort, directly adjacent to the most famous Ling Yin monastery in the suburbs of Hangzhou. We were treated to banquets with special performances. I felt particularly honored that all her guests had been friends of hers for decades, whereas I was a relatively new friend, yet also included in her very select guest list. Kevin Rudd, former prime minister of Australia, gave a lively address, and I was also given the opportunity to share my experiences in China.

As guests of this expensive resort, charging the likes of Rmb7,000 per one night stay, we have the small privilege of visiting the neighboring monastery anytime without entry fee. Otherwise, any visitor, pilgrim or tourist, would have to purchase a ticket for Rmb75 (USD12) to enter. Such an admission fee has become commonplace in China as the country has gone fully commercial. Even monks are becoming mercenaries.

"Ling Yin" literally means "spiritual and hidden". Today, the monastery is hardly hidden, and certainly has compromised its spirituality by charging a fee to the large flow of supplicants who would otherwise be glad to make substantial financial offerings anyway. Busloads upon busloads of people arrive throughout the day.

It is only 7am in the morning, and I venture to make a quick circuit walk around the periphery before exiting, as busloads of visitors are already arriving. But before the exit, there are several shops decked out with Buddhist memorabilia and mementos for visitors. While most are tourist trinkets, some items, especially cut glass or carved statues, command exorbitant prices. I suspect that such shops are commissioned to outside venders bent on cashing in on the goodwill of the pilgrims.

While tourists flood every famous site around Old Town, the West Lake, and religious or historical locations, our group is entertained to a most selective, choreographed visit, no doubt the best of what Hangzhou has to offer today. Despite the large number of cruise boats, large and small, on the West Lake, our pavilion of a boat allows us to sail around the lake in a leisurely manner with tea and other niceties served on board, prepared by the Four Seasons Hotel.

But the view, with all the car and foot traffic along the bank, is a far cry from that of 1977, a time barely at the end of the Cultural Revolution. Then there were few cars, none private, and only a few public buses, but lots of bicycles. I remember seeing young men with push carts around town, and propaganda murals and posters depicting Hua Guofeng, the successor of Chairman Mao, as well as the downfall of Chiang Qing, disgraced wife of Chairman Mao.

Today private cars, including all of the best-known brands, are choking up traffic. For the common folks there is a joke that normal people all use BMW - Bus, Metro and Walk. It takes us over an hour on a tourist bus to get from the West Lake to a specialty restaurant for lunch, as traffic comes to a stall during the weekends. Parked outside the restaurant is a full-gold Lamborghini. Some guard cones are set to protect it in case other cars might inadvertently scathe it.

I remember a joke, possibly a real event, that I read some time ago. A Saudi prince was sent to college. He wrote to his father, "Dear Dad, Berlin is wonderful, people are nice and I really like it here. But Dad, I am a bit ashamed to arrive at my own college with my pure-gold Ferrari 599GTB, when all my teachers and fellow students travel by train." The father wrote back, "My dear loving son, 20 million USD has just been transferred to your account. Please stop embarrassing us. Go and get yourself a train too."

Alibaba, one of the highest valued companies in the world, has its home in Hangzhou. Its new-gained wealth must provide the Gennie in answer to the wishes of many of China's nouveau riche class.

I have a most educational visit to Hu Qingyutang, an old Traditional Chinese Medicine (TCM) store founded in 1874. The architecture is exquisite, with carved motifs throughout the large premises. The German apprentice who introduces the concepts of Chinese medicine to us has been studying here for eight years. His systematic explanation provides the most basic, yet comprehensive, understanding for us.

Hangzhou and West Lake circa 1977 / 杭州西湖攝於一九七七年

Betsy at her birthday / 生日會上的 Betsy

Despite our group being mostly westerners, they learn to appreciate the long tradition of Chinese medicinal knowledge, including how it complements modern western medicine. There was museum display of the history of TCM as well as rooms with specimens of rare animals traditionally used in Chinese medicine, though these species are now endangered and no longer available in the open market. Visiting the dispensary and observing the pharmacists in action is perhaps the highlight of our visit. Hung above is a framed photograph of Xi Jinping visiting. It seems to ensure the correct dosage and portion are dispensed.

During a sumptuous dinner banquet, we are entertained to a performance of the Sichuan face-changing act. The solo actor performs a rendition to the awe and applause of the audience, as his smooth and precise movements change the mask on his face within milliseconds, with a swing of his sleeves or a subtle turn of his body.

In today's world, it seems such a skill could be very useful in a figurative sense. Though for me, I ponder in my mind whether symbolically Hangzhou

Ling Yin monastery morning / 晨曦中的靈隱寺
Visitors arriving / 遊客蜂擁而至
Tourist shop / 紀念品店

can be given such a facelift to the days in the 1970s, when serenity reined and people were simple yet contented.

My friend Betsy Cohen from New York chose faraway Hangzhou for her 75th birthday celebration for a very obvious reason - her respect and affinity for Chinese culture, certainly not the city's modern glamour. Her son Daniel who organized the event is Chairman of a New York bank that Betsy founded some years ago. Besides being an executive of the first order, his PhD is in Medieval Chinese Linguistics.

Historically, Hangzhou has been home to some of China's literary greats, the likes of Su Dongpo and Yufei who wrote some of the most memorable classic poems and prose of all time. Today's Hangzhou has gone through a major transformation. With prosperity, it seems that things are marching forward for the better. But perhaps it is also time to pause and think about returning Hangzhou to an epoch of the city's literary past. A renaissance in the 21st Century would be very timely.

Hangzhou and West Lake circa 1977 /
一九七七年的西湖
West Lake today / 今日的西湖

Performance at Amanfayun /
安缦法雲酒店的表演

杭州，今昔四十載

從小我就不喜歡讀結局是悲傷的故事，所以我養成先讀最後一章的習慣，若是悲劇收場的話，我就不讀這本。省下時間，也省下情緒和眼淚。

但如今即便看漫畫我都會流淚，我閱讀的每本書都像是個憂傷的故事，讓我流淚。閱讀超過二十分鐘，我的眼睛就會不禁眼濕（不是落淚，只是眼濕濕）盈眶，這真是上了年紀擾人的副作用。

我以這樣的眼睛回頭看一九七七年在杭州拍的照片，現在這些影像都以低解析度存在我的電腦裡。我邊看邊流淚，除了年紀的關係外，還有我那驟然被奪走的美好回憶。

自從一九七四年第一次進到中國以來，我已經拍了超過二十五萬張照片。只有在我重回某個地方，想比較它的今與昔的時候，才會想起那些懷舊的影像。所以，闊別了四十年後，我再次踏上杭州，已從當年年輕熱血的探險家，蛻變成了經驗豐富的探險家。

中國有句俗話說：「上有天堂，下有蘇杭」，描寫的就是中國這兩座沿海城市的美麗與祥和。也難怪，乾隆這位清朝最有文學素養、最位高權重的皇帝，會遠從首都北京六次下江南，並且每次都會在杭州停留一段時間。

HM in 1977 / HM 於一九七七年

我的紐約好友 Betsy 邀請至親好友到杭州，一同為她慶祝七十五歲生日，為此我也才有機會入住高檔的安縵法雲酒店，地點就緊鄰杭州市郊著名的靈隱寺。他們以饗宴還有特別的演出款待我們。所有出席的賓客都和 Betsy 有幾十年的交情，我雖然是個新朋友，卻也在貴賓名單之列，實在倍感榮幸。就連澳洲前總理陸克文也獲邀到場，獻上動人的致詞；我也獲邀上台和大家分享我在中國的經驗。

這間酒店一晚要價人民幣七千元，而身為賓客，我們還有一個福利，就是可以不限時段免費參觀一旁的靈隱寺。不論是來參訪或朝聖，入寺都得買上一張人民幣七十五元的門票，相當於十二美元，這樣的制度在中國走入全面商業化後已成為常態，甚至連僧人都開始作起生意。

「靈隱」字面上意即「靈性與隱匿」。但如今，靈隱寺不再隱匿，加上開始向大批到訪的信眾收取門票後，也變得沒有那麼有靈性，其實，即便不收門票，這些信眾本來就很樂意奉獻大筆的捐款。一整天巴士接著巴士為這寺廟載來大批遊客。

Lamborghini Glitter / 金光閃閃的藍寶堅尼

一大早七點鐘，我就去寺院繞了一圈，因為再晚一點就會有大批遊客湧入。離開前，我看到幾間店舖擺出為遊客準備的各種佛教紀念品和收藏品，雖然大多是小飾品，但是一些可價值不菲，特別是刻花玻璃或雕刻品。我猜這些店家都是外面進駐的，進來賺信眾的錢。

遊客一般會湧進舊城著名的景點，包括西湖和具有宗教、歷史意義的地方，但我們的團去的地方是很特別的，毋庸置疑是杭州最棒的地方。西湖上行駛著大大小小的遊艇，但是我們船上的涼亭，可以讓我們啜著茶，配著四季酒店準備的精緻小點，悠閒地遊湖。

只是，此刻眼前的風景是一片人車雜沓，與一九七七年的杭州大相逕庭，當時文革還沒真的結束。路上幾乎沒什麼車，有的也僅是幾輛公車，和很多的腳踏車。我記起那時有許多年輕人在城裡推著推車，牆上滿是宣傳的標語和海報，上面寫著關於繼任毛主席的華國鋒，還有毛主席最後身敗名裂的妻子江青。

今天私家車滿街跑，包括各種名牌車，把馬路擠得水洩不通。民間甚至流傳著一個笑話：一般市井小民都坐 BMW ——公車（Bus）、地鐵（Metro）、步行（Walk）。我們從西湖搭遊覽車，因週末交通壅塞，花了一個多小時才抵達一家特色餐廳吃午餐。餐廳外停著一輛金色的藍寶堅尼，車邊還擺著交通錐，深怕一不小心被其他車輛刮傷。

這讓我想起以前讀過的一則趣聞，或許是真有其事。有一位上了大學的阿拉伯王儲寫信給父親說：「敬愛的父王，柏林是個好地方，這裡的人都很友善，我很喜歡這裡。不過，我開著純金法拉利599GTB去上課，實在覺得有點丟臉，因為老師和同學都搭火車通勤。」父王回信說：「親愛的兒子，你的戶頭已經匯進兩千萬美元，就別再丟我們的臉，你也去弄台火車。」

杭州也是阿里巴巴總部的所在地，它是目前全球市值最高的企業之一，所創造的財富就像神燈裡的精靈對許多中國新貴心願的應許。

這趟旅程最有教育意義的一站非胡慶餘堂莫屬。胡慶餘堂是一家於一八七四年創立的傳統中藥鋪，建築偌大典雅，處處可見精美的雕塑。有一位來自德國的學徒跟我們解釋中醫的概念，他已經在這裡學習八年了。他有條不紊的解說，讓我們對中醫有最粗淺卻也全面的理解。

我們團裡雖多是西方人，但是他們學著理解歷史悠久的中藥醫學，像是中醫如何可以彌補現代的西醫。裡面還有一個中醫博物館，展出中藥的歷史，和過去曾用於中藥的稀有動物標本，然而，這些

Mural, Banner, Poster circa 1977 / 宣傳壁畫、布條、海報攝於一九七七年

動物現在都已經瀕臨絕種，無法在市場上取得。參訪藥坊觀看藥師配藥應該是這趟參觀最精彩的。藥坊上面還掛著一幅習近平參訪的裱框照片，似乎在監督正確的劑量和比例。

在奢華的晚宴中，我們欣賞著四川變臉的表演，演員臺上的一段獨角戲展現出流暢精準的動作，微微轉動身體，衣袖一振，瞬息間換上面具，博得滿堂彩。

像變臉這樣的技藝在現今社會中似乎很有用處，我思索著，杭州是否能象徵性的變臉，再次回到一九七零年代的模樣，一切祥和平靜，人民純樸知足。

我的好友 Betsy Cohen 之所以遠渡重洋，從紐約來到杭州慶祝七十五歲的生日，顯然不是因為這座城市的現代化，而是出自她對中國文化的崇敬與喜愛。她的兒子丹尼爾主辦這次的活動，丹尼爾在紐約的一家銀行裡擔任主席，那家銀行是 Betsy 多年前創辦的。丹尼爾除了是企業裡的第一把交椅外，他還有個古典中文語言學的博士學位。

杭州過去曾是中國許多文學大師的搖籃，像是蘇東坡和岳飛，他們寫出了最膾炙人口的詩及散文。今日的杭州已經歷了重大轉型，經濟的繁華，讓一切看似更將美好。或許我們也該停下前進的腳步，回到那個文學年代的杭州。那麼，是該來場二十一世紀文藝復興了。

Courtyard of pharmacy / 藥坊中庭
Xi watches over dispensary / 習近平觀看配藥

煙斗不只用來抽菸而已

A PIPE
IS NOT all ABOUT
SMOKING

Palawan, Philippines – April 30, 2018

A PIPE IS NOT all ABOUT SMOKING

I have started smoking a pipe, or to be exact, learning to smoke a pipe. My friends are alarmed and concerned. I've tried it before, but gave up, not because of health reasons, but strictly because of it being a time-consuming exercise, and at the time, my time was in short supply.

When Einstein's doctor ordered him to stop smoking his pipe, he obeyed, but only in part. He would continue to hold his pipe, even biting or symbolically puffing on it. He was heard to say, "I believe that pipe smoking contributes to a somewhat calm and objective judgment in all human affairs." The trail of smoke that followed Einstein from his home to his office and back at Princeton was famous, and following the track required no Sherlock Holmes, another person who felt naked without a pipe.

Einstein had few possessions, as one who was not committed to any worldly properties, except that of the universe. But one of his pipes found its resting place at the Smithsonian's National Museum of American History. It is an object which draws the most interest among all the displays on Physics, including groundbreaking apparatuses and instruments. The most asked-for object for display on loan from the Smithsonian is this well-used worn pipe of Einstein, even with a small hole from his bite in the mouth piece.

If Einstein epitomizes the gentile kindness and genius of a pipe smoker, Stalin perhaps provide the other extreme, with mindless persecution of adversaries and comrades alike. Known to be a pipe aficionado, even a sinister joke centers on his smoking persona.

Stalin, after a visit from a Georgian delegation, started looking for his pipe as the group headed off down the Kremlin's corridors. He couldn't find it. Stalin called in Beria, the dreaded head of his secret police. "Go after the delegation, and find out which one took my pipe," he ordered. Beria scuttled off down the corridor. Five minutes later Stalin found his pipe under a pile of papers. He called back Beria – "Look, I've found my pipe." "It's too late," Beria said, "half the delegation admitted they took your pipe, and the other half died during questioning".

As Nobel pipe smokers go, if Einstein represents the scientists then Bertrand Russell no doubt highlights the literati. He admitted to smoking his pipe all day long, except at meetings and during his sleep. Russell lived to be 98, with over 75 years of being an active pipe smoker, trumping Hemingway, another Nobel laureate who also had an affinity for the pipe. Russell's indulgence included recounting coolly how smoking once saved his life. While on an airplane, Russell sat in the smoking section. It crashed in the water off the Norwegian coast. All the passengers in the non-smoking section were drowned, whereas those in the smoking section survived by swimming to shore.

Even military commanders, including general Patton, smoke the pipe. The most iconic, however, being the "I shall return" General MacArthur. His pipe was never far from his lips, even as he waded ashore at Leyte Island in the Philippines. His corn cob pipe is parallel of that used famously by Popeye, the sailor man. While MacArthur may

HM with pipe / HM 抽著煙斗

have picked the choicest tobacco from the Philippine highlands, Popeye's selection has been said to include a certain special stash, or plainly speaking, marijuana, but concocted as his most potent spinach. One strip illustrated a shipment of "pure spinach" arriving in the dark of night, straight from Bolivia.

Popeye, however, did not rule as the king of pipes within the comic world. In the adventure of Tin Tin the star character Captain Haddock, another sailor, should take that honor. Surveys revealed he is the most popular character within the series, ahead of Snowy in second place. Tin Tin, the namesake journalist-explorer only came in third.

For Captain Haddock, his alcohol, in particular Scotch, and his pipe are never far from his reach. He even once had a boy villain's bullet shoot his pipe off his lips. His choice of pipe and tobacco has become a point of speculation among pipe smokers. The final verdict is that he smokes a Billiard pipe, and most likely puffed British Navy Flake, a traditional tobacco flavored with rum and a touch of honey, preferred by many sailors. But not a few opined that he must be smoking a cruder form, rope! Which of course was made of hemp in those days, and marijuana is in fact a type of hemp.

Hemp and hash in pipes may be what many of the ethnic minorities in remote

China smoked. Some of these hill tribes were known to grow opium as well as other potent crops. But what fascinates me is that many women among these people also smoke a pipe, the Yi, the Lisu, and the Deng. One old Lisu lady who just passed away this year at the age of 92 even shared her pipe with me. She was known to down two bottles of white liquor and an endless stash of tobacco each day.

As for yours truly, this explorer is contemplating the days ahead on an armchair as an ex-explorer, smoking his pipe. That however, may still be twenty years away. I always say I am both busy and lazy. To handle the former, I need to be super efficient, creating more time for the latter. And the latter is where the style comes into play, including adding a few special touches to our many projects.

Recently, I have tried to slow down, allowing more time for being lazy with style. I took up walking my two Westie's (my sidekicks, like Tintin's Snowy), I write letters to close friends using a fountain pen, I occasionally practice using my left hand. I even got rid of my two iPhones and opted for a Huawei, learning anew how to use the new device. Selective efficiency I call it. And I turned to smoking a pipe. None of the above can be rushed.

On seeing me with a pipe, Dr. Bleisch told me he used to smoke one too, during his days as a PhD candidate and later as a post-doc at Caltech. That's how I found out I needed more pipes than one, ideally seven, one for each day of the week. On a visit to California, my

Sherlock Holmes / 福爾摩斯

Stalin with pipe / 叼著煙斗的史達林　* Attribution: Bundesarchiv, Bild 183-R80329 / CC-BY-SA 3.0

close friend Paul Lee, a physicist also with multiple pedigree degrees from Caltech, revealed to me that he too, used to smoke a pipe. He shouldn't have to give up, as Amy his wife, another Caltech grad, is a pioneering scientist on cancer research.

When asked about the danger of cancer, my standard answer is, "It takes time to develop cancer, and I am almost 70 and I am just now starting". Over lunch, Amy briefed me on her latest research, imminent of a breakthrough. Next stage is clinical tests of her new drug and treatment. She would need around USD5m to take it to human trials, perhaps meaning 1m for each individual as guarantee. I suggested to her that I may become one of her next specimens, a worthy candidate to receive the 1m. I can only wish her breakthrough is for real and in time.

Martin, a Hong Kong close friend, has so far bought me some of my finest pipes, all the way from Milan, as he was heading to his family skiing trip in Switzerland. The same Amorelli brand of pipe has been presented to dignitaries like Pope John Paul II and Bill Clinton, with the latter receiving a huge one in the shape of a saxophone, which he enjoys playing.

Martin had never smoked a pipe and bought one also for himself, so we can both be learners at the same time. He later bought two more for me, both Italian ones, including a Castello

Aristocratica, with signed inscription by its founder Carlo Scotti and burnt edges. Very few of these are crafted. I must also introduce Amy to Martin, though he may not need the USD1m.

As I was puffing on my latest and favorite pipe addition, I felt just like an aristocrat. I watched the haze rising heaven bound. An image suddenly came to my head. I recalled seeing a group photo of Swiss priests of the St Bernard Mission at their mission house high on the Tibetan plateau. Despite the rarefied air, every single priest had their pipe on their lips or in their hand. God must have consented, with a smile.

HM with pipe writing / HM 叼著煙斗寫作

Lisu smoker / 抽著菸的傈僳族人   Deng smoker / 抽著菸的僜族人

Yi smoker / 抽著菸的彝族人

煙斗不只用來抽菸而已

我抽起了煙斗，或應該說開始學抽煙斗。身邊的朋友驚訝又擔心。其實以前我就抽過，只是後來沒抽，不是因為健康的考量，而單純的只是這事件太花時間，當時，我每天的時間都不夠用了。

醫生告誡愛因斯坦要戒掉抽煙斗的習慣，他聽進去了，但是只聽了一半。他還是習慣性的叼著煙斗，好像真的在抽菸那樣。他曾說：「抽煙斗好像可以讓人冷靜思考，客觀判斷關於人間的事。」在愛因斯坦來回家中和普林斯頓大學辦公室的這條路上，彷彿飄著一道煙，要追蹤這道煙不需要福爾摩斯，而福爾摩斯恐怕也是一位沒有煙斗拿在手裡就會覺得渾身不對勁的人。

愛因斯坦除了研究宇宙外，對任何世俗財物並不感興趣，因此私人物品並不多。但是史密森尼國立美國歷史博物館卻陳列了他其中的一支煙斗。館中展出的各種他用過具開創性的物理學設備和儀器，但最受人矚目卻是這支煙斗。這支常被使用的老煙斗，煙嘴還被愛因斯坦咬出了一個小破洞，但是它卻仍是大家最想要向這家博物館租借的展品。

若愛因斯坦的溫柔仁慈和天才是抽煙斗者的形象，那麼史達林代表的就是冷血迫害敵我的另一個極端。他也愛抽煙斗，但他抽煙斗的形象成了惡毒笑話的素材。

故事是這樣的，會晤完喬治亞代表團之後，一行人走下克里姆林宮走廊，史達林卻遍尋不著他的煙斗。他把凶狠的祕密警察首腦貝利亞叫了進去，「去追代表團，揪出是誰拿走我的煙斗！」史達林命令道，貝利亞快步跑去。五分鐘後，史達林在一疊紙下找到了他的煙斗，於是他叫回貝利亞，「看，我找到了！」。「太晚了」貝利亞說，「代表團一半的人都認了他們拿走你的煙斗，而另一半的人在嚴刑訊問過程中都死了。」

以諾貝爾獎得主的煙斗族來說，愛因斯坦是科學家的代表，伯特蘭・羅素無庸置疑就是文人的代表。羅素自己也承認，除了開會和睡覺外，其他時間都抽著煙斗，抽了七十五年，活到了九十八歲，遠超越另一位也是一樣愛抽煙斗的諾貝爾獎得主海明威。羅素很喜歡淡然地講著抽煙斗曾救過他一命的故事。有一次搭飛機，羅素坐在吸菸區，後來飛機在挪威海岸墜海，非吸菸區的乘客都溺斃了，只有吸菸區的乘客得以游上岸而倖存。

不僅文人學者抽煙斗，連巴頓將軍這樣的軍事領袖都抽，最具代表性的人物是講過「我還會再回來！」的麥克阿瑟將軍。他總是煙斗不離嘴，即便在菲律賓萊特島涉水上岸時，也是叼著煙斗。他抽的玉米穗軸煙斗跟大力水手卜派著名的煙斗一樣。或許麥克阿瑟會選擇來自菲律賓高地的上等菸草，而據說卜派有特別的煙草，講白一點就是大麻，這是他最強的菠菜。甚至還有一幅漫畫裡面提到一批「純菠菜」在深夜裡直接從玻利維亞運送過來。

不過，卜派還算不上是漫畫界的煙斗王。《丁丁歷險記》的明星人物阿道克船長才配得上這個頭銜，他同樣也是水手。調查顯示，他才是這個系列中最受歡迎的角色，再來是狗兒米魯，記者兼探險家丁丁只位居第三。

阿道克船長總是酒和煙斗不離，特別是蘇格蘭威士忌。他還曾經被小混混拿槍打掉他叼在嘴裡的煙斗。一直以來，大家都在猜測阿道克船長到底用哪種煙斗、抽哪種菸草，結論是直柄式煙斗，而菸草最有可能是英國海軍薄片煙，一種混有萊姆及少許蜂蜜的傳統菸草，這個口味深受水手喜愛。但是也有不少人認為，他抽的應該是一種更為粗糙的菸草－繩子！在當時繩子是用麻做的，而大麻也是一種麻類植物。

大麻和哈希是許多中國偏遠地區的少數民族抽的菸草。一些山區部落還會種植鴉片以及其他一樣強效的作物。但是最令我覺得有趣的是，這些部落中很多女性也抽煙斗，像是彝族、傈僳族和傣族。曾經有一位傈僳族婦女還跟我分享過她的煙斗，她今年以九十二歲的高齡辭世，她可是每天都會喝掉兩瓶白酒，煙也抽個不停。

而老實地說，我這個探險家現在正思索著，當未來有一天成為前探險家的時候，我會坐在扶手椅上，叼著煙斗。但，那可能是二十年後的事了。我常說，我又忙又懶。面對忙碌，我必須有極高的效率，才能有更多時間慵懶。而慵懶才有時間塑造某種風格出來，或許可以為很多項目加入獨特想法。

近來，我試著放慢腳步，有更多時間用我的風格慵懶。我開始帶著我的兩隻西高犬出門散步，牠們是我的隨從，就像丁丁身旁的米魯一樣。我也開始用

HM sharing Lisu pipe / HM 抽著傈僳族煙斗

鋼筆寫信給好友，有時還練習用左手寫字。我甚至把兩支 iPhone 換成了華為，重新學習使用新的裝置。我將這些稱作有選擇性的效率。然後，我開始抽煙斗，這些事都是急不來的。

畢博士見我抽煙斗，跟我說起他念博士以及在加州理工學院讀完博士後在那裡做研究的時候也曾抽過。看來一支煙斗恐怕不夠用了，最好有七支，剛好一週，每天抽一支。記得有一次到加州拜訪好朋友 Paul Lee 李隆生，他是一位物理學家，在加州理工學院拿了好幾個學位，跟我說他以前也抽煙斗。他真的不需要戒掉，因為他的太太 Amy 是研究癌症的先驅。

每當有人問我難道不怕罹癌，我的答覆都一樣：「罹癌需要時間，而我都快七十了才剛開始抽煙斗。」吃午餐時，Amy 跟我聊了一下她最新具突破性的研究。下個階段要進入臨床試驗，而人體實驗需要五百萬美元，或許意思是每個人要一百萬當作擔保。我跟 Amy 建議，說不定我可以成為她的實驗對象，一位非常值那一百萬的對象。我只能期待她突破性的研究可以實現也能及時到來。

我現在最好的幾支煙斗，都是一位香港的好朋友 Martin 趁著全家到瑞士滑雪時順道從米蘭帶回來的。教宗若望保祿二世和柯林頓都曾收過 Amorelli 的煙斗，喜愛吹奏薩克斯風的柯林頓還收過一支薩克斯風形狀的 Amorelli。

從未抽過菸的 Martin 自己也買了一支，我們兩剛好可以一起研究。他後來又買了兩支給我，都是義大利製，其中一支 *Castello Aristocratica* 上面刻有創辦人 *Carlo Scotti* 的簽名，邊緣還有燒痕，非常稀少的物件。雖然 *Martin* 可能用不著那一百萬美元，但我一定要把 *Amy* 介紹給他認識。

抽著我最新的跟最喜歡的煙斗，我活像個貴族。看著白煙裊裊往天際飄去，心中頓時浮現出一個畫面，回想起一張聖伯納宣教任務中，瑞士牧師在青藏高原上宣教屋前拍的團體照，儘管空氣稀薄，但是每一個牧師嘴上或手上都有一支煙斗，我想，上帝一定是帶著微笑點頭允許的。

St Bernard Mission in Tibet / 西藏聖伯納宣教任務團

HM with Castello pipe / HM 抽著 Castello 煙斗

布
拉
瑪
普
特
拉
河
源
頭

TO THE SOURCE OF
THE BRAHMAPUTRA

Brahmaputra Source, Zhongba, Tibet –
June 3, 2018

TO THE SOURCE OF THE BRAHMAPUTRA

Point of arrival at traditional source

Latitude: 30.272233N (30°16'20"N)

Longitude: 82.263832E (82°15'49"E)

Elevation: 5312 meters

Time: 11:54 am

Date: June 3, 2018

New source data from Satellite Images (for reference)

Latitude: 30°22'06"N

Longitude: 82°03'20"E

Elevation: 5319 meters

Now we have descended to a more "comfortable"
4794 meters to set our camp. It is barely seven
hours since I reached the source of the Brahmaputra,
a source long established by locals as a sacred glacier

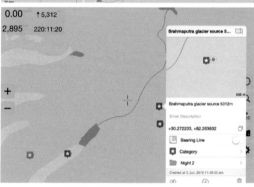

Route from road to source / 溯源路線
Satellite data at source / 源頭的衛星資料

fed river and for a long time endorsed by the Chinese government, as well as foreign geographers, as the official source. This is the sixth major source of an Asian River I have reached.

But what is considered official, traditional, even religious, has only measured significance for an explorer. It seems strange that as a younger person some years ago, being accurate, scientific and definitive seemed to count a lot to me in my pursuit of excellence. Now at a more senior age, on the margin of finishing my seventh decade, things begin to move into a blur. Exacting details have come to seem somewhat irrelevant.

Perhaps complementing my failing eyesight, not to mention my declining energy, I have become more abstract and philosophical, and also more traditional. I've been known for defining new sources over the last two decades. But this time, I made an exception and went against my own tradition and decided to endorse the tradition of the local Tibetans.

Recent remote sensing data published by experts from Beijing, as well as our own processing of current satellite images, have revealed a yet longer source nearby, at Angsi glacier. I have deliberately decided to lead my team to the traditional source, the Chemayungdung glacier. The two points are less than 30 kilometers apart as the crow flies, the traditional source in Zhongba county and the other in neighboring Burang County.

The debate about where the Brahmaputra river begins has baffled more than a generation of geographers and explorers, spanning over a century. There are multiple theories, based on exploration of the region, measurements of quantity of flow, or related as legends and hearsay from local Tibetan nomads. The Indian scholar Swami Pranavananda made an exhaustive research, both on the ground in the 1930s and from scrutinizing previous literature of

other explorers who had pursued the same in the region.

Citing works by Chinese geographer Klaproth, and foreign explorers like Dutreuil de Rhins, D'Anville, Henry Strachey, Ekai Kawaguchi, Graham Sandberg, Nain Singh, C.H.D. Ryder and Cecil Rawling, all famous for their work in western Tibet, he wrote a long chapter in his book "Exploration in Tibet" to refute the assumption and conclusion by stellar famed explorer Sven Hedin, and maintained that the Brahmaputra source is at the Chemayungdung glacier. Angsi glacier, while also mentioned being massive as Chemayungdung, was considered secondary.

At noon today, we were above 5,300 meters looking across at the Chemayungdung glacier source of the same elevation that is still a few kilometers away across a deep ravine above a glacier lake and alpine marshes. On a straight line, where

Glacier source and lake / 冰河源頭與湖泊

I stood is approximately 7.6 kilometer from the tongue of the glacier that feeds the 1.9 km long glacier lake, which in turn is the source lake of the Brahmaputra. Such measurements are made through a Vector map I use on a Galileo app in my iPad.

A stone tablet, roughly half a meter tall, was anchored to the ground, near some old, torn prayer flags and a few meters from where we parked our vehicles. On it is inscribed in Chinese, "Source of the Yaluzangbu," meaning Brahmaputra. Here is where we set up our own length of prayer flags, released the sacred longda paper offerings, and took our group photo.

We literally drove to this source, easy compared to the previous five river sources that I have visited, to which we had to drive, ride horses or yaks, and hike before reaching our goal. This time around, there was a dirt road leading up to this point, finished last year, one year after a Chinese scientific expedition set foot here and established this point, looking down on the glacier lake, as the source of the Brahmaputra.

The feeder Chemayungdung glacier is approximately 7 km in length, and an entire range of high peaks behind form the Himalayan range separating Nepal from Tibet of China. This glacier is the longest and largest of three glaciers adjacent to each other, each feeding the lake below. Our original LatLong and Altitude measurement was done from space. Now we are finally on the ground with the Chemayungdung glacier source within a short distance.

Two weeks before, in a rush to leave from our Zhongdian Center for this expedition, we spent an entire day packing and making sure everything was in order for a month-long journey. Provisions, tents, medical kit, vehicle spare parts, precautions against altitude sickness in the form of oxygen tanks, air-concentrator machine, compression chamber - everything was finally in place. We even brought longda, or Wind Horse cards, paper slips inscribed with the form of a horse carrying special offerings to deities, set on its way when released to the wind. These were for dispersing at high mountain passes and at the source itself.

Long strings of the five-colored prayer flags were also put aside for attaching to special sacred sites, as we had done at other river sources we had attained. But by my own error, I neglected to bring our CERS flag for the all-important group picture at the river source! Thus for the first time our photo at the source has no display of the CERS emblem, another inadvertent adherence to my newly-gained philosophical outlook.

In the past, another tradition was to open a bottle of Moet Chardon to celebrate the occasion. This time however,

CERS team at source /CERS 團隊於源頭處合影   HM directed by image / HM 用衛星導航找路

High camp / 高原上的營地
Tracking with maps and digital images /
地圖與數位影像協助探源

it was omitted, not by design but by negligence. I had a metal hip flask that contained leftover Louis XIII brandy from my centenarian pilot friend Moon Chin, given to me when I visited him a few months ago in San Francisco. I took it out and toasted myself. Though no champagne, it cost around $4,000 USD a bottle, multiple times that of Moet Chardon. The ease with which we arrived here took away some of the usual emotion and drama. The Louis XIII however, did take me higher, beyond the already high altitude.

The dirt road breaking off from the main road from Lhasa to Kailash is totally obscure. We were fortunate to have along 48-year-old Nanda, a local who is the party secretary of nearby Yuelai Village. He was dispatched by the local government to accompany us as our guide, having been to the source three times before. Without Nanda, we could never have identified the branch of the road, let alone followed the 65 Km track to the source. Before the road was completed last year, this distance would have translated into three days on horse back, each way.

There were a few camps of nomads scattered around, who had already moved their livestock, mainly sheep, goats and yak, up to a high camp. Now that we were into June, the summer season on the plateau had started. On the way out, we made sure to stop and interview the "first" family on the Brahmaputra. It was actually two tents and two families, living next to each other. They *were conducting cooperative livestock herding, staying at this high camp for up to three months, planning to move down to their winter home near Puyang Township at the end of September.*

Nanga Chomo, the lady of the first tent, greeted us and invited us into her tent. Soon goat and sheep droppings, from a dry pile, were added to the stove, and she went about boiling tea for these unexpected guests. In a matter of fifteen minutes, milk tea was served while we sat on the right side of the tent, a place reserved for visiting guests.

My camera was trained on the wonderful face of her daughter, barely three years old. Nanga, at thirty-three years old, also had a son at five years old. We were also eager to pick out a few pieces of the nomads' utilitarian objects as memorabilia to grace our own yak and nomad camp exhibit back at our Zhongdian Center. As they needed everything they brought to camp, we ended up only purchasing a hundred dollar's worth, or about two catties, of freshly sheered wool. At local market, the same price would pay for half a kilo of wool.

On this day, the goats were being sheered. They were separated from the sheep as goat's cashmere command a much higher price than sheep's wool. The men were busy rounding up their herd for this yearly routine. Each year their goats, over three hundred strong, could yield over 10,000 RMB worth of cashmere.

Someone would come by to collect the wool, which was destined to be made into the highest grade cashmere, given these were high-altitude goats valued for their finest quality wool. At Rmb100 per half kilo, the added value to finished product would produce multiple returns, perhaps ending at branded stores in fashion capitals of the world. I thought of having leading wool merchants like Loro Piana come here to source their raw materials from such an exotic location in the Himalayas. Imagine, a cashmere sweater knitted from goats grazing the scanty pasture of the Brahmaputra source at the dizzying altitude over 5000 meters. Can't get more romantic than that for a product story.

It seems most appropriate that our next stop, within less than half a day's distance, is Mount Kailash, the most sacred mountain for Tibetans and Hindus alike. Fresh from the source of the Brahmaputra, five members of our nine-person entourage decide to make the circumambulation (kora) pilgrimage. Miraculously, they manage to complete the circuit in just one long, long day, leaving before sunrise and returning by late evening. It seems a grand finale to complement reaching the Brahmaputra source - a double-crown achievement.

I had already hiked the 53-kilometer circuit kora during the auspicious Year of the Horse in 2002.

Nanga's baby girl / Nanga 的小女兒

On such a special year, one circuit equates to 13 circuits in a normal year, and likewise the merit gained is multiplied. So I opt to keep that record and instead spend a day to explore the border town of Burang near the frontier with Nepal and India. Though the Indus source is nearby to the north of Mount Kailash, it must be left to the future, as the Lord of Kailash would find me too greedy if I were to challenge two major river sources on one single trip.

Our road ahead into Ngari, Xinjiang and the Silk Road beyond is still long. But for the moment, I can lie back and contemplate a little. While the rest of Asia and coastal China are baking in the summer heat of 35°C to 40°C, we've been operating in snow, hail and high winds at sub-zero temperature during many nights of camping out in our effort to get here. Pictures of myself clad in thick down jackets and multi-layer clothes should give my friends on the receiving end, even those hiding in alpine resorts, a moment of chill.

Inside first family tent / 第一戶人家的帳篷內

Nanga in her tent / Nanga 在她的帳篷內

布拉瑪普特拉河源頭，仲巴縣，西藏　二零一八年六月三日

布拉瑪普特拉河源頭

舊源頭
緯度：北緯 30°　16’　20”（30.272233N）
經度：東經 82°　15’　49”（82.263832E）
海拔：5312 公尺
時間：上午 11 點 54 分
日期：二零一八年六月三日

衛星影像資料顯示的新源頭（供參考）
緯度：北緯 30°　22’　06”
經度：東經 82°　03’　20”
海拔：5319 公尺

我們來到 *4,794* 公尺較為「舒適」的海拔紮營。攻抵布拉瑪普特拉河源頭到現在還不到七小時。這條河自古就是當地人眼中由冰川所孕育出的神聖河流，他們所定出的源頭早已獲得中國政府和外國地理學家的認定。這是我溯源亞洲第六條大河的源頭。

對探險家而言，官方、傳統或甚至宗教上的認定，它的重要性不是絕對的。說也奇怪，年輕時我追求卓越，凡事要求精準、科學、明確，如今年紀大了，都快七十了，事情開始變得模糊。追求確切的細節好像已經不再是那麼重要。

或許眼睛越來越差，體力也是，我變得更能接受抽象，變得更哲學，也更傳統。過去二十幾年來，我最為人知的是探索河流的新源頭。但這次，我決定顛覆自己一貫的作風，開了特例，決定替藏人傳統所認定的源頭背書。

根據北京專家所公布的最新遙測資料，以及我們近期的衛星影像分析，源頭應該是位於更上游處的 *Angsi* 冰川。但我決定帶著團隊朝著位在傑馬央宗冰川傳統的源頭前進，位於仲巴縣的傳統源頭和緊鄰普蘭縣的新源頭相距不到三十公里。

源頭究竟位於何處，過去一百多年來一直困擾著無數的地理學家和探險家，他們透過實地調查、測量水量或連結起西藏當地遊牧民族的傳說和傳聞，提出了各種理論。印度學者普拉納瓦南達（*Swami Pranavananda*）對此進行了詳盡的研究，他在一九三零年代進行了實地探訪，更爬梳了過去探險家在此的實地探源資料。

普拉納瓦南達在他的《探索西藏》（*Exploration in Tibet*）一書中，援引了中國地理學家 *Klaproth*，及外國探險家 *Dutreuil de Rhins*、*D'Anville*、*Henry Strachey*、河口慧海、桑德伯格（*Graham Sandberg*）、*Nain Singh*、賴德（*C.H.D. Ryder*）和賽西爾羅林（*Cecil Rawling*）這些研究藏西地區著名人物的論述，他用一長篇駁斥著名探險家斯文赫定（*Sven Hedin*）的假說和推論，並認為布拉瑪普特拉河的源頭應是傑馬央宗冰川。雖然有人認為 *Angsi* 冰川與傑馬央宗冰川的大小差不多，但前者被視為是次要的。

今天中午，我們越過了海拔 5,300 公尺，這裡能看見位處同樣高度的源頭傑馬央宗冰川，但相距還有好幾公里遠，要越過冰川湖上的山溝和高山沼澤才到得了。目前我們離冰河舌的直線距離約 7.6 公里，這條冰川會注入一座長達 1.9 公里的冰川湖，而這座湖正是布拉瑪普特拉河的源頭。這些測量數據都是我用 *iPad* 上 *Galileo* 應用程式 *Vector* 地圖得來的。

源頭處的立了一塊約半公尺高的石碑，一旁飄揚著歷經風霜的經幡，這裡離我們停車的地方只有幾公尺。石碑上刻著幾個中文字：「雅魯藏布江源頭」，也就是布拉瑪普特拉河。我們在這裡揚起經幡，往空中撒龍打，拍攝團體照。

我們可以說是開車直接開到源頭，比起過去五個河流的探源來得輕鬆許多，以往我們都必須經歷開車、騎馬或犛牛，步行跋涉，才到得了目的地。而這一次，出現了去年才開通的直達源頭的泥土路，這條路是中國的科學探險隊來到了這裡，定出布拉瑪普特拉河源頭一年後才開的，冰川湖就在下方。

傑馬央宗冰川這條支流約有七公里長，背後重山峻嶺綿延成喜馬拉雅山脈，形成尼泊爾與中國西藏之間的分界。傑馬央宗冰川是注入冰川湖鄰近的三條冰川中最長最大的一條，之前我們曾用衛星定出這裡的經緯度和海拔，但是這次我們終於親臨傑馬央宗冰川源頭的不遠處。

就在兩週前，我們急著從中甸中心出發，花了一整天整理行李，確定備妥一個月行程中所需的東西。食物、帳篷、急救包、車子備用零件、減緩高山症的氧氣筒、氧氣濃縮器、壓力艙。最後一切就緒。我們還帶上了印有馬匹圖案的龍打（風馬旗），隨風撒向天空，準備要在隘口、源頭地獻給神明。

Sheering goat / 剪山羊毛
Combing goat / 梳理山羊毛

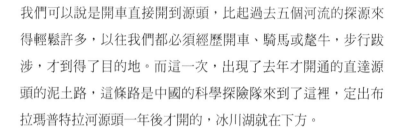

我們還準備了長串的五色經幡，好在聖地懸掛，如同過去我們在其他河流源頭所做的一樣。不過這次我卻忘了帶 CERS 旗子！這也是第一次我們的團體照中沒有出現 CERS 的旗幟，無意中發生的事確剛好符合我最近的哲學觀。

過去的另一個傳統就是在登抵源頭時開一支酩悅香檳慶祝。但是這次沒有這麼做，並不是刻意不帶，而只是完全忘了。我的不鏽鋼酒壺裡裝的路易十三白蘭地，是幾個月前到舊金山拜訪好友陳文寬時他送我的。我拿出酒壺敬自己一杯。雖然沒有香檳，但是這種白蘭地一瓶可要 4,000 美元左右，是酩悅香檳的好幾倍。這次溯源雖然毫不費力，但也少了以往那種情緒和戲劇性。路易十三下肚後讓我情緒高漲，甚至高過了現在的海拔。

泥土路是由從拉薩到岡仁波齊峰的主要道路所分岔出來的，很不容易找。幸好有 48 歲的當地人 Nanda 帶路。他在 Yuelai 村附近擔任黨書記，因為曾到過源頭三次，所以當地政府派他來當我們的嚮導。如果沒有 Nanda，我們大概找不到這條路，更別說還要沿著 65 公里的小徑來到源頭。去年，路還沒開通時，到源頭來回恐怕得在馬背上各花上三天的時間。

高原上可以看到零星的游牧民族的帳篷，他們已經帶著自己的牲畜，大部分是綿羊、山羊和氂牛來到高地。現在進入六月，夏季已經來到高原。回程時，我們不忘到布拉瑪普特拉的「第一戶」人家拜訪。這裡有兩個帳篷，兩戶人家比鄰而居。他們在這裡的三個月裡，一同合作放牧，預計九月底再遷回帕羊鎮過冬。

Nanga Chom 是第一個帳篷的女主人，出來歡迎我們並邀請我們進帳篷。山羊和綿羊的糞乾堆成一疊，她拿了幾塊放進火爐燒水準備茶水招呼我們這些不速之客。十五分鐘後端出酥油茶給坐在帳篷右側的我們，右側是給來訪的客人坐的。

我拿出相機對準小女孩可愛的臉龐，她是 Nanga 的女兒，還不到三歲。今年三十三歲的 Nanga 還有個五歲的兒子。我們原本想要挑一些遊牧民族使用的工具，帶回中甸中心擺在犛牛和遊牧民族的營地展覽裡。但是這些都是他們帶來營地的生活必需品，所以最後只買了約兩斤的現剪羊毛，一百塊錢人民幣。同樣的價錢在當地市場只能買到半公斤。

那天恰好是替山羊剪毛的日子，綿羊和山羊必須分開剪，因為山羊絨可以賣上更好的價錢。男人們忙著集結羊群，準備開始這個每年的例行公事。每年這三百多頭產出喀什米爾的山羊，可以替他們賺進人民幣一萬塊以上的收入。

會有專人來收購這些羊毛，然後製成最高級的喀什米爾羊絨，因為這些高海拔山羊毛的品質是非常好的。半公斤人民幣 100 元，層層加工的生產過程讓價錢翻了幾倍，成品還可能出現在世界各大時尚重鎮的名牌店。我想過，說不定可以讓知名的羊毛商像 Loro Piana，直接到充滿異國風情的喜馬拉雅山取原料。想像一下，在超過海拔 5,000 公尺令人暈眩的高度，山羊在布拉瑪普特拉河源頭稀疏的草原上吃著草，而這件喀什米爾羊絨毛衣正取自這些山羊。有比這個還更浪漫的產品故事嗎？

我們下一站安排的很恰當，到岡仁波齊峰不到半天路程，這座山是藏人和印度教徒眼中最神聖的神山。剛剛才從河流源頭下來，我們九個隨行隊員中，有五人決定到岡仁波齊峰「轉山」。奇蹟似的，他們一天之內完成轉山，天亮前出發，黃昏後回來。這趟轉山無非是在我們抵達源頭後另一個完美的休止符，兩大目標一次完成。

早在二零零二年適逢馬年吉祥年時，我就已經完成這 53 公里的轉山，在那個吉祥年轉山一圈等於平常轉 13 圈，也就是說，能得到的福報加倍了。我決定保留這個紀錄，所以利用這一天跑到尼泊爾和印度邊境的普蘭鎮探險。雖然印度河的源頭離這裡不遠，就在岡仁波齊峰北側，但是還是留待下次吧，因為如果一次就登抵兩條大河的源頭，岡仁波齊峰的山神可能會覺得我太過貪心。

距離新疆的阿里及深入絲路，雖然還有很長的一段路，但是這一刻，我可以放輕鬆沉思。現在亞洲的其他地方，包括中國的沿海地區，正處於 35°C 到 40°C 的酷暑，但是為了抵達這裡，我們卻必須在許多個紮營的夜裡，歷經零下的風雪、冰雹和強風。我把穿著厚重羽絨外套和好幾層衣服的照片寄給朋友，就算是在高山避暑的他們應該也會覺得冷吧！

High Himalayas / 喜馬拉雅群山聳立

從後門進入不丹

BACK DOOR
INTO BHUTAN

Phari, Tibet – June 18, 2018

BACK DOOR INTO BHUTAN
Or are we still in China?

"You are fortunate, dealing with us People's Liberation Army," the PLA officer said politely. "The Gong An are on their way and they may be more strict and harsh," he added with a smile. But I fully understand what is behind that smile; it means business. Better settle now than later, before the police arrive. At least now we can have a graceful exit.

We have just travelled across much of Tibet and southern Xinjiang, going through over 80 police check points within one month, and certainly we would not want another engagement with the Gong An. Practically all check points in Tibet are staffed by Tibetan policeman and those in Xinjiang by Uighur, a great surprise for me. They are very professional and usually quite polite. However, each of these security check points may mean 15 minutes to an hour of delay to our trip, and this one at an international border may mean days, if they should turn suspicious about our presence.

Fortunately, all three soldiers now approaching us are from Yunnan, and six out of nine on our team are from that same province. To neutralize the situation, I mention to the officer that two members of our team are veterans of the PLA, having fought in the war between Vietnam and Chi-

na in the early 1980s.

The tone behind the politeness of the officer is obviously a soft threat. He has two junior officers with him. Everyone is dressed immaculately, with dignified uniform, as if ready for a ceremonial parade. At an international border, proper looks and protocol must be the norm, to represent their country, though the capital may be thousands of kilometers away.

The young but distinctive looking officer is no doubt of higher rank, with a desert-colored camouflaged greatcoat. It is necessary, as day-time temperature can suddenly drop dramatically if a cloud should move in. At such elevations, we are susceptible to even summer snowstorm and sub-zero weather.

Indeed, the Army always carries more weight and muscle than the police, and not only in the weapons and military gear that they carry. Thus, they may feel no need to flex their muscles. How unlike some countries, which cannot stop displaying their strength outwardly even though everyone already knows they are strong.

"You must move out of here," the officer insists. We are pleading to stay for the night. After all, the sun is setting and there may be only another hour of light, and our camp was set up a few hours ago. "This is unsettled territory, and the Bhutanese army sentry is just a bit further down the valley," he adds. I take particular note of his term, "unsettled", rather than "disputed". Such measured language speaks a lot about the difference between rhetoric and politics.

"But, but... we have our border permits, and the other PLA soldiers I ran into this morning said it was ok to drive

in on this road," I protest. "Their jeep ran off the road and we towed it back up before I asked to come off the main road," I explained. "Yes, you can come in for a look, but not to stay for the night," the officer further emphasizes his request, now sounding more like an order.

"You see those tents of the nomads. They are both Bhutanese and Tibetans. They both use this valley as summer pasture. This area of the border has not been settled as belonging to Bhutan or China yet." he points his finger at a few yak-hair tents spread out in the valley as he speaks. Valley

Our tents among nomads / 與遊牧民族的帳篷搭在一起

perhaps is an exaggerated description. There are high snow mountains on both sides, and the narrow pasture is sandwiched in between with a stream running through the middle.

"By the way, please allow us to check through everyone's mobile phones. We need to make sure nothing sensitive is recorded," the officer adds, after I agree to pull camp and leave the area. There are trenches dug around the hill, though we saw no installation of artillery. Would writing about this incident be considered sensitive and revealing of a state secret, I wonder silently? Would discussing such matters create another political fiasco like what hap-

Valley inside snow mountain / 雪山中的山谷

Route ending in Jiu Wu valley /
到 Jiu Wu 谷的路線

pened at the nearby border of Doklam last year? But I have more immediate issues to take care of.

Within a matter of twenty minutes, all our gear, five small tents and one big dining tent, are packed away and back in the cars. I want to get out before the police arrive, in case more complications develop. We might be escorted out of the mountains, or even detained. I have handled such situation many times, but I certainly know my limits.

While the officer in charge had asked each of us to hold up our ID card in front of our face for a photo for "memory," he ultimately forwent checking our phones. Actually, my camera had recorded much of the nomads, especially the Bhutanese ones, in their camps. My innocent face must have done the trick.

We quickly wind back through all the switch-backs of the dirt road over which we had come, over a high pass of 4659 meters and back to the main road to Phari. It is barely ten kilometers away, though the mountain road has taken us some twenty kilometers into the valley. On my Vector Map, as well as on satellite images, the border between China and Bhutan was shown at the high pass, before we dropped down into the valley.

That was exactly what I had come for; to have a look at a remote and lit-

tle-known international border, perhaps even having a photo taken of myself standing next to a border marking stone, which I had done at many well-demarcated borders of China. But here there was no border marker to be found.

As we exit a simple gate at the end of the side road manned by a Tibetan, three men in Bhutanese costume are setting up their camp by the road. With loads of baggage, these are the traditional traders who occasionally came with their caravan of horses or yaks across the mountain passes from Bhutan into Tibet.

While there are no diplomatic relations between Bhutan and China, such age-old civilian trading has been maintained. Bhutan is the only country within China's orbit that has no diplomatic relationship with China. But that situation may soon change, after twenty-five rounds of informal negotiation and consultations to settle border disputes over the last two decades. Such dialogues have been cordial and peaceful, and may one day lead to formal recognition of each other.

Even last year's tension at Doklam near Yadong was handled peacefully, despite India, the "big brother" of Bhutan, intervening and escalating the dispute. Today, despite the military presence, things have turned quiet and everything seems to have returned to normal along Yadong's border with Bhu-

Bhutanese caravan traders / 不丹的商隊
Downtown Yadong / 亞東市區

tan and Sikkim, which we have visited over the last couple days. Even the border trade with India's Sikkim has gone up at the border trading post near Yadong. My last visit to Yadong was in 1999 when it was a quiet border town. Today it is a bustling small city with many modern buildings, restaurants, shops and finely paved roads.

I suspect such disputed, not necessarily confrontational, areas can become pawns on the chess board of international politics. While China has a record of conceding to neighboring countries territory it has claimed as its own, there could be bargaining before such trade offs. It is to the advantage of China, with such a huge area, to act as the nice guy with smaller and weaker neighboring nations. It certainly does not want to be portrayed or viewed as a bullying big neighbor.

I hope that the current impasse with Bhutan is just temporary posturing, trading off one piece of territory for another perhaps at a more strategic location. What may be crucial for one nation may be less important for another, and such trade offs can be based on political, economic or military importance.

Road toward Bhutan border / 通往不丹邊境的道路

Foothill Chomolhari campsite /
紮營在卓木拉日山的山麓

The area here at Yadong has been used by trade caravans, religious pilgrims and political missions for centuries. Numerous explorers used this route as entry point into Tibet from the Indian continent. The scholar Professor Tucci passed through this route no less than four times, the last being 1950 just before the PLA marched into Tibet.

British expeditionary forces led by Colonel Younghusband fought their way to Lhasa between 1903 and 1904 through exactly the same route, leaving a bloody path of massacre of the ill-equipped Tibetan army with the decisive battle at nearby Gyantse. The fortressed town at Gyantse was the third largest settlement in Tibet before 1949. Throughout history, Tibetan aristocrats from Lhasa or Gyantse would intermarry with royalty from across the border

Modern Tibetan traveller / 現代西藏旅人

in what was the Kingdom of Sikkim. Such courtship abruptly ended with the 1962 India-China border war. Sikkim was absorbed into a state of India in 1976.

Even during the Chinese Nationalist era and well into early Communist rule in the 1950s, when China and India were undergoing a short-lived honeymoon, dignitaries and government officials used Yadong as transit point to and from Tibet, offering the shortest distance to the nearest ocean. Yadong was also the exit point for many Tibetans in the late 1950s and early 60s as they fled into exile, first to India and then continuing on to many areas of the world.

Though we have to pack and leave the "unsettled" border between Bhutan and China, we are lucky to manage interview with two nomad families of Bhutan before the PLA locates us. One can distinguish their tents from those of the Tibetans from the Chinese side by a flag they fly outside their tent. The white flag with three lines of color,

Traffic jam near Phari / 帕里鎮附近遇上塞車

Tibetan moving camp in tractor / 藏人用拖拉機移動營地

red, blue and yellow, signifies that they are from Bhutan, being the flag they commonly fly outside civilian home. The Tibetan nomads herding their livestock here fly a Chinese red flag with stars. I have a feeling that such measures of patriotism and nationalism may be choreographed, part of posturing and staging to show that both countries have traditional grazing rights in this particular summer pasture for their livestock.

Bienmo is the Bhutanese lady tent owner we visit. She is most gracious and stops milking their yaks as we approach. Leading us into her tent, she quickly puts fuel, yak dung, into the fire and soon we have a hot cup of milk tea to sip as we sit and chat. From her, we learn that this valley is called "Jiu Wu." Bienmo is 49 years of age whereas her son Bienjau is 29.

They also hire two helpers during the summer busy months, as they own over 100 yaks. From the number of calves at camp, life must be prosperous, and their future bright. Herding the yaks and milking the cows twice a day during the three months they camp here can be quite time consuming and exhausting. So far, they seem to live peacefully right next to Tibetan nomad camps within ear-shot of each other, and their language seems to be largely the same. Perhaps they feel closer to each other, physically and emotionally, than toward their respective leaders far away in the capital.

Inside Bienmo's tent is a nicely set up altar with Buddhist statues and deity images, oil lamps and an assortment of other religious paraphernalia. At the base of the altar I notice a mug adorned with a picture of the current Fifth King of Bhutan and his Queen. Apparently, this mug is used as an ornament of respect rather than for drinking. Without taking too much of her time while her yaks are waiting to be milked outside, we thank her and head back to our camp. That is when three PLA officers arrive on motorbikes to check on us.

While there seems to be no immediate tension and confrontation at this border region between Bhutan and China, here is also where the most sacred mountain of Bhutan stands, astride the two sides of the two countries. Chomolhari is a majestic goddess of the Himalayas. Standing at 7325 meters elevation, it has watched over the people of both Bhutan and China in kindness for millennia. With her blessing, I hope the peaceful relationship between the two countries and its people will continue into the future.

Bienmo's tent / Bienmo 的帳篷

從後門進入不丹

還是我們還在中國？

「你們很幸運遇到我們解放軍」，解放軍官客氣地說。「公安還在路上，他們可就沒那麼好說話了。」他面帶微笑說。但是，我完全明白這個微笑背後的意思。最好在公安趕到前解決，至少現在我們還有機會可以優雅地離開。

我們剛剛走遍西藏和新疆南部，一個月裡經過了 80 個檢查哨，實在真的不想再跟公安打交道。西藏所有的檢查哨都由藏族公安負責，新疆則是維吾爾族，這倒是令我頗為吃驚。這些公安都非常專業，也很客氣。但是，每經過一個檢查哨，我們的行程就會被迫延後十五分鐘到一小時，而在這個國際邊境，若公安對我們有疑慮，可能就要耗上好幾天。

幸好盤查我們的三名解放軍都是雲南人，我們九人團隊裡就有六個雲南人。為了緩和局面，我告訴那位軍官，我們有兩個隊員是解放軍老兵，曾在一九八零年代初打過中越戰爭。

這位軍官禮貌的語氣顯然是個軟威脅，跟在他身旁的兩個下級軍官穿著整潔端莊，彷彿準備要去參加閱兵典禮。在國際邊界正式的穿著和禮儀一定是常態，因為代表的是自己的國家，雖然首都可能在千里之外。

這位年輕軍官的服裝與其他人不同，披著漠色迷彩大衣，軍階明顯較高。在這裡，白天若開始有雲，氣溫可能驟降，所以需要大衣。這麼高的海拔，即便是夏天，也有可能遇上暴風雪和氣溫零下的天氣。

光從他們身上帶的武器和裝備，就可以看出他們比公安更有分量，也更有力量，所以他們並不會刻意地展現。不像有些國家不斷向外界展現他們的力量，即便大家早就知道他們已經很強大了。

「你們不能在這裡停留！」軍官很堅持說道。我們懇請他們讓我們在這裡過夜，畢竟太陽已經快下山，再一小時天就要黑了，而我們也在幾小時前就搭好了營帳。「這裡是未界定區域，不丹的駐軍就在山谷不遠處。」他接著說。我特別注意到他說「未界定」而不是「具爭議」，從這樣謹慎的措辭，就能明顯地發現用詞巧妙和政治語言的差別。

Bienmo milking yak / Bienmo 擠氂牛奶

Bienmo with dried yak yoghurt / Bienmo 拿著氂牛乾酪

「但是但是……我們有邊境許可證，今天早上遇到解放軍說我們可以開進這條路。」我抗議說。「在我要求離開這條幹道前剛好遇到他們的吉普車開出車道卡在路邊，我們還幫忙把車拖上來。」我解釋著。「你們可以進來看看，但是不能過夜。」軍官再次強調，現在聽起來更像是個命令。

「你看這些遊牧民族的帳篷，他們是不丹人和西藏人，到了夏天都會進到山谷放牧。但是，這個地區還沒劃清是屬於不丹還是中國的領土。」他邊說，邊指著散落在山谷地的幾個氂牛營帳。說山谷似乎有些牽強，因為兩旁就緊鄰高聳的雪山，這片狹窄的草原就夾在中間，草原中還有溪水流過。

最後我答應拆掉帳篷離開。軍官接著說：「對了，請讓我檢查你們每個人的手機，我們必須要確保沒有什麼敏感的東西被記錄下來。」山丘附近有幾條壕溝，但是我們並沒有看到任何火砲設施。我暗自想著，把這件事寫出來會被視為敏感的事，算不算洩露國家機密？討論這些事情，又會不會引發像去年洞朗邊界的政治事件？不過，我沒時間多想，還有更緊急的事情要先解決。

短短二十分鐘內，我們把所有的裝備、五個小帳棚和一個大的用餐帳篷收好，搬上車。我想在公安趕到前離開，避免更複雜的問題發生，因為我們可能會被護送下山，甚至可能被拘留。這種狀況我處理多了，當然知道我的限度在哪裡。

那位軍官叫我們拿著身分証舉在每個人的臉前面拍照「留念」，他最後並沒有檢查我們

Tent altar with dried yoghurt / 帳篷內神龕上供著乾酪
Bienjau at 29 / 二十九歲的 Bienjau
Bhutan King & Queen image on mug / 印有不丹國王和皇后肖像的馬克杯

的手機。我手機裡確實錄了不少遊牧民族，特別是不丹遊牧民族，在他們的營地裡。或許是我這張無辜的臉奏效。

我們很快沿著來程的 Z 型泥土路，通過海拔 4,659 尺的隘口，回到通往帕里鎮的主要道路。這裡離帕里鎮只有十公里，但是這條山路卻帶我們開了二十公里進到山谷。在進山谷前，我的向量地圖和衛星影像，都顯示中國和不丹的邊境就位在這個隘口。

這正是我來的目的，要看看這個遙遠且鮮為人知的國際邊境，或許還可以和界碑合影，之前我到過中國許多劃界清楚的邊境，都會和界碑合影。但是這裡卻看不到界碑。

我們在小路的盡頭通過了由藏人把守的簡易哨口，看到了三位穿著不丹服飾的男子正在路邊紮營，一旁放著一堆行李，他們是傳統的商人，有時會帶著馬隊或氂牛隊從不丹的山路進到西藏。

雖然不丹和中國沒有邦交，但是長久以來民間仍維持著貿易的往來。不丹是唯一一個鄰近中國，卻沒有和中國建交的國家。然而，這情勢可能會改變，過去二十年來，兩國為了解決邊界爭議，已經進行了二十五次非正式的談判和協商。兩邊的對話都算友善和諧，或許有一天兩國都能承認彼此。

鄰近亞東的洞朗，儘管曾有不丹「老大哥」的介入讓爭議擴大，但是去年的緊張情勢終於和平的落幕了。雖然現在仍有軍隊在，但是一切平靜。前幾天我們才剛到過與不丹和錫金接壤的亞東，一切也都回復往常，邊境貿易也開始了。還記得一九九九年我第一次到亞東時，它還是個安靜的小鎮；如今它已經變成熱鬧的小城市，許多現代的建築物林立，也有許多餐廳商店和鋪設很好的道路。

我覺得，這樣的爭議雖然說不上是衝突，卻讓這些地區成了國際政治棋盤上的棋子。雖然中國宣稱他們將自己擁有的領土歸還給鄰國，但是退讓前免不了要談條件。中國幅員如此遼闊，若能善待鄰近較弱小的國家，對中國有好無壞，畢竟中國也不想被外界描繪成只會欺壓鄰國的大國。

我希望不丹現在的僵局只是暫時的，割捨一小部分領土，換取另一個更具有戰略地位的地方。對一個國家可能很關鍵的，對另一國卻未必，而這樣的取捨可以從政治、經濟或軍事上做考量。

亞東這個地方幾個世紀來，都是馬隊經商貿易、信眾朝聖和政治活動的要地，也有許多探險家利用這條路線，從印度進入西藏。學者圖齊教授就曾不下四次走這條路線，最後一次是在一九五零年，正好在解放軍進入西藏前。

一九零三年到一九零四年間，由榮赫鵬上校指揮的英國遠征軍，也經由這條路線一路攻到拉薩，在江孜一役中，大舉殲滅了裝備不足的西藏軍隊。這個要塞小鎮在一九四九年之前，是藏族第三大的居住地。自古以來，拉薩和江孜的西藏貴族會跨越邊界與當時的錫金王國結親，這樣的政策在一九六二年中印邊境戰爭爆發後嘎然而止，而錫金在一九七六年則成了印度的一省。

從一九五零年代國民政府到共產黨統治早期，中國和印度曾短暫地和平相處一段時期，政府要員和官員更將亞東當作往返西藏的中繼站，因為那裡離海最近。到了一九五零年代末、六零年代初，亞東也成了許多西藏人逃亡印度，再輾轉走向世界各地的起點。

雖然不得不離開這個不丹和中國「未界定」的邊境，但是我們很幸運能在解放軍找到我們之前拜訪了兩戶不丹游牧民族。我們可以從他們帳篷外懸掛的旗子區別他們。民間常把白底配上紅、藍、黃三色線條的旗子插在屋外代表他們來自不丹；而藏族則是懸掛中國的五星紅旗。我認為，這樣的愛國表現也許是刻意的，一部分是為了宣示兩國傳統上都有在這片夏季草原放牧的權利。

Bienmo 是我們拜訪不丹營帳的女主人，非常親切，我們走近時，她馬上停下手邊擠奶的工作，帶我們進帳篷，馬上將犛牛糞乾加到火爐中，不久後我們手中就握有一杯熱騰騰的奶茶，邊喝邊聊天。聽她講我們才知道，原來這個山谷叫「*Jiu Wu*」。*Bienmo* 今年四十九歲，有一個二十九歲的兒子 *Bienjau*。

由於養了超過一百頭氂牛，到了夏天最忙碌的時候，他們還請了兩位幫手。從小牛的數量可以看出，他們生活富足，未來一片光明。他們到這裡紮營的三個月裡，每天都要趕放氂牛、擠兩次奶，非常耗時勞累。雖然和藏族比鄰而居，他們卻能和平共處，而且彼此幾乎沒有語言的隔閡，比起在遠方的國家領導人，他們在生活和情感上或許更親近彼此。

Bienmo 在營帳裡精心擺了一個神龕，上面有佛像和其他神像，油燈及各式各樣的宗教用品。我還注意到下面放了一個印著不丹現任第五世國王和皇后肖像的馬克杯，顯然這是出自對皇室尊敬的裝飾品，而非拿來使用的。我們不想佔用 *Bienmo* 太多時間，因為外面還有氂牛需要擠奶，向她道謝後，我們就回到了自己的營地。這時三名解放軍正好騎著摩托車到來盤查我們。

這個不丹和中國的邊境看似沒有立即的緊張和衝突，而這裡也是不丹神山橫越兩國高高聳立的地方。雄偉的卓木拉日神山是喜雅拉馬山的王妃神山，站在海拔 7325 公尺之高，千年來一直慈悲地守護著不丹和中國的居民。在祂的庇佑下，我祈禱這兩個國家和他們的人民能夠持續和平友好的關係。

Sacred Chomolhari / 神聖的卓木拉日山

清邁的咖啡餐廳

A CHIANG MAI
CAFÉ-RESTAURANTS

Chiang Mai, Thailand – July 10, 2018

CHIANG MAI CAFÉ-RESTAURANTS
And a barber's repertoire

"Oi? But that's the same name as my daughter," I questioned the coincidence. "No, Koi, with a K in front," answered by my barber while clipping short my hair on top. Her English was sketchy and scratchy, almost minimal, but we managed to strike up a conversation.

As usual, I am not having a haircut because of the hair, but for chatting, and at a convenient time. Besides, I always get bored being fixated to a chair for anything longer than 15 minutes, a trait developed since my elementary school days. Multitasking my haircut becomes a solution, thus chatting turns into interview.

Dancing tattoo of birds / 手上刺的鳥舞動   Koi checks on her art piece / Koi 檢視她的作品   Armful of art / 滿手的藝術

And on this day, my hair is seriously long, getting in the way of my sight. It's been over two months since my last cut, for free in Palawan by my staff, and in between I had a five-week expedition in Tibet.

Koi is exceptional, a stylist in the full sense; style in both her near skin-head haircut, and in an armful of tattoo. Birds in flight constantly flash in front of my eyes crossing from one side of my head to the other as the backs of her arms move across my vision. Then there is her choice of decorations on the wall, rock and Harley Davidson posters. Given her looks, I would not be surprised if she had such a machine, or was aspiring to have one.

Momentarily, with the center part of my hair clipped upward, she danced around my head with her scissors and tattooed arm performing what I imagined as a pirouette, as if choreographed by a seasoned performing artist. Soon, hair fell like snowflakes around me. Every now and then, she would stop, stand back and bend her head back and forth, seemingly in appreciation of a piece of art sculpture, just as an artist would check and measure her unfinished piece. Lastly, she combed my top hair downward, giving it a final trim right above my eyes.

Koi is no regular hairdresser. She doubles as a waitress, which is perhaps her primary profession. Her one seat

Koi rechecking / 再檢視一次   Koi's one seat shop / 只有一個座位的理髮廳   Barber sign outside restaurant / 餐廳外的理髮廳招牌

barbershop is tucked away behind glass doors at the corner of a street-side café-restaurant in an obscure back street of Chiang Mai, a city in northwestern Thailand. I saw a barber sign, popped in for a look, and decided to come back after my visit to another destination a short distance down the street.

I was strolling by on my way to have lunch at a 125-year-old historic building, the 137 Pillars House now turned into a classic hotel. It was formerly the northern headquarters of the East Borneo Company, and played in the book Anna and the King, later turned into more than one popular film, with the King of Siam (modern day Thailand) portrayed first by Yul Brynner and later by Chow Yun Fat. First known as Borneo House, it was built at the end of the 19th century by the son of Anna Leonowens, the real British tutor of the King of Siam, who inspired the book by Margaret Landon.

The lunch, Thai cuisine at 137 Pillars, was my first upon arriving in Chiang Mai on a direct flight from Hong Kong. Over the next day and a half, I tried numerous street snacks, mobile café, a church coffee shop, and several restaurants. That included a packed room serving Italian food operated by a retired Thai officer with an Italian wife and a father-in-law chef. The father passed away a couple of years ago, but the flavor was still authentic.

Market by river / 河岸邊的市場
Pagoda at night / 晚上的佛塔

The Japanese restaurant next to Asia Books store was sizable, unlike tiny places around Tokyo. As it was acceptable to a full table of Japanese seated next to me, I reasoned it must also be the real thing. The Shangri-la hotel next to the Astra Residences where I stay served up a daily Dim Sum buffet, always my first choice for lunch. Even the upstairs Nepali joint above the Himalayan trinket store by the flower market offered a nice diversity of ethnic dishes. The raised platform seats overlooking the busy street below always seemed to be occupied by a few hippie-type backpacker girls.

Flower market at night / 晚上的花市

Mobile café / 行動咖啡車
Church coffee shop / 教堂咖啡廳

Perhaps the most unusual meal was my very first time visit to a kosher restaurant, just steps away from the Astra. The lady owner came to Chiang Mai over ten years ago from Israel. Sababa is set up as a not-for-profit eatery to serve Jewish expats and tourists who either live here or travel to distant Chiang Mai. In fact, a card on the table depicts the restaurant is actually operating at a loss. Yet the service it provides justifies it, with the food most delicious and inexpensive.

The menu offers Israeli and Thai kosher food, prepared under the supervision of Rabbi Yosef Kantor. The restaurant is also where Friday services are held. After a wonderful lunch, I left with four bottles of wine from Israel that I would take along to my next destination in Mandalay, to be enjoyed on our HM Explorer boat.

For getting around, I employed Udong who operates an old yet clean trishaw. Udong casts a long shadow around the streets of Chiang Mai, being over seventy years old. His age can be a draw back as I felt bad watching him worked away on his peddles. So I often opted to dismount when there was a slight

Street snack cart / 路邊餐車
Tuk Tuk drivers at rest and at meal /
休息吃飯中的嘟嘟車駕駛

slope like when going up a bridge. But having him in the evening allows me to randomly make night pictures around the city.

A quiet stroll along the bank of the Ping River lined with small boutique shops and hotels is a nice contrast from the long and busy stretch of Chiang Mai's night market. At various corners of the market, small crowd of locals and foreign tourists gathered around a portable TV or two to view the evening broadcast of the latest world cup soccer game beamed from Sochi. The occasional cheers of "Oos…!" and "Ahhs…!" gave indications of a goal or a miss. There seemed much at stake on mobile phone betting to add to the excitement.

For a moment, the focus here seemed to have eclipsed the tense scene that the world was also following intently in a town not far from Chiang Mai. Less than 200 kilometers away, twelve teenage students and their soccer coach were trapped in a flooded cave in nearby Chiang Rai. The tension would come to end with the joyful news today of the successful rescue of the entire Wild Boar team, after a 17 day ordeal.

Long shadow of Udong /Udong 長長的影子

Going back to my special haircut, in casual conversation, I found out that Koi learned to cut hair over six months before opening her small shop two years ago in the back of the family restaurant. On an average day, she may have three customers, whereas the café and restaurant catered to a much larger customer base.

At the end after about 30 minutes, I had one of my best moments of any haircut, watching this "artist" made her finishing touches. The bill came to 100 Baht, a meager three US Dollars. I left 20 Baht as tip, and she provided a parting smile. Before I walked out, she gave me a business card with eleven little circled scissors printed on the back. There is an electric shaver sticker on the first circle. After ten cuts, you would reach the red circle to redeem a free cut.

Chiang Mai seems a long way to go for a haircut, even one by Koi. But perhaps in years ahead, I may just reach that red circle if this special cut would bring me back time and time again. And for now, every time I use the "Cut and Paste" icon on my computer writing app, it reminds me of that very special cut in faraway Chiang Mai. And coming back to Chiang Mai for a haircut seems a good excuse that fits the persona of an explorer.

清邁的咖啡餐廳

和一位多技能的理髮師

「*Oi*？那不就和我女兒同名？」我問了一下這個巧合。「不是，是 *Koi*，開頭是 *K*。」理髮師一邊剪我的頭髮一邊說道。她只會說一點點英語，但是，我們還是有辦法聊天。

一般我去理髮都不是因為頭髮太長，而是去聊天，當然也要剛好有空。此外，我實在無法坐著不動超過十五分鐘，這是從小學就養成的習慣，所以我只好邊剪頭髮邊做其他事情，於是聊天就成了訪談。

那天，我的頭髮已經過長，遮到了眼睛，上一次剪髮已經是兩個月前了，還是我的員工在巴拉望免費替我剪的，中間五週的時間我還去了西藏探險。

Koi 很特別，是一位非常有型的髮型師，她的風格展現在很短的髮型和一手的刺青。當她的手臂從我眼前移動時，彷彿那刺青的鳥也在空中飛了起來從我眼前閃過。牆上掛著她選的裝飾品，有搖滾樂和哈雷機車的海報。從這些看起來，如果她真的有台哈雷機車或者她嚮往擁有一台，對我來說一點也不奇怪。

就在我的頭髮往上夾起後，Koi 的剪刀和刺青開始在我頭上舞動起來，彷彿跳著單腳旋轉舞曲般，髮絲很快的如同雪片般掉落在我身邊。不時，她會停下來往後站一步，搖頭擺首地前後移動，彷彿在仔細欣賞一件雕塑品，猶如藝術家會細心審視即將完成的作品一樣。最後，她放下我那被夾起的頭髮，一番梳理後在我眼睛上方做了最後的修剪。

Koi 並不是一般的髮型師。她還是個服務生，這個或許才是她的正職。她的理髮廳只有一個座位，就隱身在清邁巷弄裡一家街角咖啡廳的玻璃門後，一個位在泰國西北的城市。當我看到理髮招牌時，先進去看了一眼，然後決定先到同一條街不遠處瞧瞧，再轉回來剪髮。

我經過這家理髮店時，正散著步前往 137 幢柱洋房去吃午餐。這是一棟擁有 125 年歷史的建築，以前是東婆羅洲公司的泰北總部，現在已改裝成一家古典的飯店，還出現在後來改編成兩部知名電影的《安娜與國王》一書中，在第一部電影中，尤·伯連納飾演暹羅國王，第二部的國王則是周潤發。這棟建築最初被稱作 Borneo House，由暹羅國王的家庭教師安娜·李奧諾文斯之子，在十九世紀末所建，李奧諾文斯也是啟發瑪格麗特·蘭登寫出這本名著的人。

137 幢柱洋房的泰式料理，是我從香港直飛到清邁後的第一頓午餐。接下來的一天半，我嚐過好幾家路邊攤、咖啡車、教堂咖啡廳還有幾家餐廳，包括一家由一位泰國退役軍官和義大利籍太太及岳父一起開的義式餐廳，岳父也是這裡的廚師，生意非常好。雖然岳父在幾年前過世，但是口味依然很道地。

亞洲書店隔壁的日本料理店蠻大的，不像在東京那麼小。我的隔壁坐了一整桌的日本客人，因此我猜想這家餐廳應該夠道地。我入住的香格里拉飯店就在 Astra Residences 旁，每天都供應港點自助餐，這一定是我午餐的首選。連花市旁的喜馬拉雅飾品店樓上，也提供各種民俗風味料理的尼泊

爾餐廳。店裡的挑高平台區可以看向樓下繁忙的街道，這區總是坐著幾位嬉皮女背包客。

我吃過最特別的一餐應該是一家符合猶太飲食戒律的餐廳，這是我第一次嘗試，餐廳距離 Astra 並不遠。十幾年前，老闆娘從以色列來到清邁。Sababa 是非營利的小館，服務外派到此的猶太人和遊客。桌上卡片寫著餐廳其實還在虧錢，但是提供的服務並沒有打折扣，食物非常的美味又不貴。

在 Sababa 可以吃到符合猶太飲食戒律的以色列和泰式料理，烹調由 Yosef Kantor 拉比把關，這裡週五也會舉行禮拜。吃完美味的午餐後，我在店裡買了四瓶以色列紅酒，準備帶到我們的下一站曼德勒，在 HM Explorer 上享用。

我雇了 Udong 的三輪車，好讓我可以機動性地到處閒逛，他的車雖舊，卻很乾淨。Udong 長長的影子就映在清邁的街上，他已年過七十，看著他奮力踩著車，讓我很過意不去。所以只要遇到上坡，

像是上橋，我都會主動下車。不過，晚上有 Udong 在，我才能隨意地在城裡拍攝夜景。

沿著許多小商店和旅館的河岸靜靜地散步，這種感覺與清邁的夜市有很大的反差，夜市很長也很熱鬧。在夜市裡好幾個角落，當地人和外國遊客圍著一兩台可攜式電視，觀注從索契轉播的世足賽，從此起彼落的「哇！」、「唉！」，就可以知道球進了沒。很多人透過手機下注，讓賽事更加刺激。

此刻，賽事沖淡了全世界都在關注的事，離清邁不遠，情況十分危急。就在不到兩百公里外，十二名足球隊學生和他們的教練，因為溪水暴漲，而被困在清萊附近的一個洞穴內。最後終於傳來好消息，野豬足球隊在經歷了十七天的磨難後，全員獲救，大家終於可以鬆一口氣。

回到我在理髮時的閒聊。我後來才知道，兩年前 Koi 在家庭料理餐館後面開理髮廳前，她花了半年學習理髮。平日她一天大概有三位客人上門剪髮，而咖啡廳和餐廳的客人就多上許多了。

歷經三十分鐘快要結束前，我經歷了理髮過程中最感動的一刻，看著這位「藝術家」為作品做最後的修飾。剪一顆頭一百泰銖，折合美金才三塊錢，我多給了 Koi 二十泰銖當作小費，她滿面笑容送我離開。在我走出店門前，Koi 給了我一張名片，背面有十一個剪刀圍成的小圈圈，第一個圈圈裡已經貼上了一張電動剃刀的貼紙，剪十次，就可以集滿紅色圈圈，免費剪一次頭。

即使是特地找 Koi 剪髮，跑一趟到清邁理髮似乎太遠了。但是未來我可能會再回來，或許有一天會集到一個紅色圈圈。現在我每次使用電腦上的「剪下、貼上」，我都會想到遠在清邁那次特別的理髮經驗。回到清邁剪頭髮這藉口，也挺符合一位探險家的性格。

參與過五場戰役的百歲飛行員

CENTENARIAN PILOT
WHO FLEW IN FIVE WARS

Milwaukee, Wisconsin – July 23, 2018

CENTENARIAN PILOT WHO FLEW IN FIVE WARS
From Missionary pilot to Mercenary pilot

(All black & white photos used with permission of Felix Smith)

His fingers are long, slender and frail. Felix Smith held the pen firmly and with slow but determined movement he autographed his book for me. "For How Man, withanks for all of the good things you have contributed to the history of CNAC and CAT. Felix." So it reads now on the inside cover page of the book, China Pilot, flying for Chiang and Chennault. That's the first time I saw someone short-cut the words "with thanks". For Felix however, his life had no short-cuts, but instead was long and distinguished.

A later edition of the same book has the title China Pilot, Flying for Chennault during the Cold War. Chiang Kai-shek was cut off, as he became less and less relevant in Asia and the world. This is not just another book among a very long list of books written by pilots who saw action in battles and wars. According to Felix, the Smithsonian Institution Scholarly Press, which published the later version, chose the book as one of ten best war aviation history books.

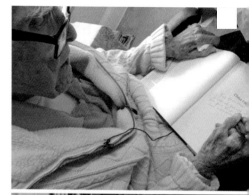

These same fingers signing the book must once have danced on the keyboard of the baby grand piano now sitting idle in the living room, covered with two layers of cloth. During Felix's childhood growing up in Milwaukee, his father was a head music teacher. That influence certainly must have rubbed off on young Felix, since he learned to play both the violin and piano.

Not far from the piano by the corner window, boxes of papers and old photographs surround a bed transforming the space into Felix's bedroom. Having turned 100 earlier this year, age and frail condition have imposed constraints on movement, and Felix has moved the bed from his second-floor bedroom to the ground floor, at a corner of the living room.

It was also these same fingers which held firmly to the steering wheel inside the cockpits of a large array of airplanes as Felix flew through darkness, thunderstorms and sprays of gunfire during five wars in Asia. "In total, I have flown over thirty thousand miles in an airplane," Felix confided to me.

First mail bag to Warlord Ma Pu-fang / 給軍閥馬步芳的第一個郵包

As a young man, Felix joined CNAC, China National Aviation Corporation, in 1945, flying the HUMP during the final days of World War Two. That was followed by a long stint after the War with CAT, Civil Air Transport, started by General Chennault of Flying Tiger fame. In fact, CAT had nothing civil about it. Instead, it was run much like a military logistic and cargo airline.

With CAT, Felix flew on the Nationalist side during China's Civil War from 1945 to 1949, ferrying troops and ammunition back and forth as conflict dragged on throughout the Mainland. Such flights continued after the Nationalist retreat to Taiwan, after which Felix and other CAT pilots conducted dangerous covert flights into the Mainland during the early years of the PRC. Throughout much of the Cold War and through several hot wars, CAT was the civilian proxy

Felix with young guard by St Paul / Felix 和年輕的護衛與聖保羅號合影

airline for the CIA, flying junkets into much of Southeast Asia. Similar airline outfits were named Air America and Air Asia.

Between flying for CNAC and CAT, Felix became a pilot for the first ever Christian Missionary Airline in the world, flying a war surplus C-47 turned into a cargo plane for relief and medical supplies. The plane was christened St Paul, after the first missionary disciple. On its fuselage was painted a red heart with orange flames around the edges, inscribed with bold lettering underneath, "Lutheran World Mission."

Felix was hired by Reverend Daniel Nelson, a missionary who started this odd airline. Besides St. Paul there was St. Peter, another C-47, but missing an engine. "We rob Peter to pay Paul," Daniel confided to Felix, explaining how they cannibalize one plane for spare parts to keep the other in the air. Daniel was killed with his family some

CAT flight over Shanghai / 民航空運班機飛越上海
Troops boarding flight to Manchuria / 準備飛往滿州的部隊

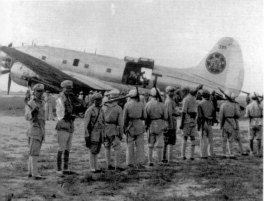

months later in a Macao Airways flying boat, when four passengers who were bandits tried to waylay a shipment of gold in the plane's cargo hold. Amid the mayhem on board, the pilots were shot in the cockpit and the plane plunged into the sea.

The Korean War followed, and Felix continued his flying career with CAT, which Felix in his book often referred to as "the company." Many of the flights were carrying military personnel or supplies, all contracted by the US Army. When the French Indo-China War began, CAT began flying covert missions in Southeast Asia, which was the beginning of a long relationship with the CIA, which Felix called "the customer."

The flights to service the French forces in Indo China lasted many years, at times flown in big planes like the C-119 called the Flying Boxcars, right up to the siege of Dien Bien Phu. Indonesia was another theater where CAT saw action, airdropping supplies to support an uprising in an attempt to unseat then President Sukarno, whom the US suspect to have communist leaning.

Lastly was the Vietnam War, from the mid-fifties to the mid-seventies, with most of the action for CAT in Laos, when CAT was again contracted by the CIA. There were also smaller contracts and lesser skirmishes in between, like ferrying Hmong hill tribe fighters in an attempt to harness the communist rise in Asia. These missions, while small, were no less significant and were just as dangerous to a flyer as the five recognized "Wars" listed above.

In one incident, Felix had just finished training for flights into Tibet to airdrop Tibetan Khampa guerilla trained by the CIA to harass the PLA after the Dalai Lama went into exile in India. William Welk, his colleague at CAT, pioneered most such flights. But in 1960, just as Felix was about to be dispatched in a B-17 bomber for this long-range mission out of Bangkok in full darkness, the US government stopped all covert flights after a U2 spy plane was shot down over the Soviet Union and its pilot Gary Powers was captured.

Several times during our conversation about his clandestine missions, Felix put his finger to his lips with a secret grin and whispered, "I kept my mouth shut, but we all kind of knew what each other was doing." This happened whenever he was recounting their work for "the customer" as he called the CIA. Occasionally, there would be a slip of the tongue and he would simply say CIA. Each time he realized it, he again put his finger to his lips.

But Felix flew more than military missions. Once he flew a full load of sheep from New Zealand to Mainland China for the Nationalist's Agriculture Ministry. These were to be used as new stock and studs to revive the local livestock after the War. Later, CAT, operating from Taiwan, pioneered a passenger service called Mandarin Jet in parallel to its military cargo service, more or less as a cover for the covert missions.

"This book I wrote is really about all my pilot friends, not so much about myself," he reiterated more than once. But reading through it, one cannot but be carried along by someone who was quite a maverick during the heady days of the Cold War. It was a far cry from today's automated flying machines in which a fighter pilot does not even have to see the enemy aircraft before engaging to shoot it down with the push of a button.

"Some of our fellow pilots were such great flyers that when I saw them fly, I wanted to resign," Felix said. I asked about the father of a common friend, Harry Cockrell. "Oh, I knew Harry Junior since he was born. And Senior is one of those very fine pilots, and also a gentleman with excellent manners, always immaculately dressed," Felix recounted. I asked about Moon Chin, another common friend, who turns 105 this year. Felix was all praise and said Moon was one of those best pilots that Felix admired. "I've learned a lot about Chinese through Moon", he added.

CAT was stationed in Taipei during the 1950s and 60s. "In those days, I had a Chinese cook, and I told him 'Cook no lap sap!' meaning no trash" Felix said. "But I could tell just from the smell coming from the kitchen that he was cooking up some nice Chinese dishes, not for me, but for his other friends," Felix recounted with a smile in his face.

His book recounted several major airplane disasters. One was the downing of a Cathay Pacific flight near Hainan Island in 1954. The commercial flight was shot out of the air by two Chinese Air Force jets. Among the passengers was Len Parish, one of the CNAC pilots,

Delivering sheep from New Zealand / 從紐西蘭空運綿羊

and his family. His wife Fran and daughter Valerie survived the crash and were rescued from a life raft, while Len and his two sons went down with the plane.

I have known Valerie for many years as we met at the annual CNAC reunion in San Francisco. While the fiasco triggered massive media coverage at the time, few knew or noticed the final reparation and apology that China made afterward, admitting to a mistake. Felix thought the fighter pilots might have mistaken the first three letters of Cathay for CAT, the American-funded airline.

Felix also exposed another mysterious loss of a CAT C-46 passenger flight operating around Taiwan. It was in 1964 and during the time of the Asian Film Festival hosted in Taiwan. Returning from the south, the plane made a stop at Makung, an off-shore seaport island with many military installations less than a hundred miles from the Mainland. Piloting the plane was Benji Lin, a seasoned captain with fourteen years of flying experience. Benji graduated from the Chinese Air Academy and was son-in-law of Tiger Wang (Wang Hsu-ming), commanding general of the Chinese Air Force.

Boarding the plane in Makung were several US military advisors and two Chinese. One was a Navy lieutenant, a radar expert attached to the Makung shipyard. He was accompanied by a retired naval officer turned businessman. They had no luggage and the lieutenant was on a 72-hour leave. They carried two confidential radar manuals as hand-carried items. The plane continued to Taichung and picked up the group of celebrity passengers with their entourage.

A US air attaché expert was allowed to inspect the crash site since there were US military advisors among those who died. Contrary to the Taiwan government crash report, the expert reached a highly disturbing conclusion. He surmised that the plane had been hijacked and made to turn toward the mainland, commencing a flight path back and forth, before finally plunging into a rice paddy.

To make a complicated espionage story short, the account by the air attaché described the pilot being shot in the head. And the two confidential radar manuals, which escaped detection, had been cut out inside in the shape of a gun, sufficient to hide two .45 pistols. But for security reasons, this report was never released, as the Nationalist government did not want to raise panic with a report of a hijacking during a sensitive time when relations with the Mainland were volatile. Instead, CAT took the blame in a cover up that accused the airline of poor maintenance of the airplane.

Among those who died in the crash was Asia movie tycoon Loke Wan-tho. I wish I had uncovered all these intrigues of the CAT crash earlier, as I could have related all of these details to an old and dear friend. Lady McNeice, who passed away in 2012 at the senior age of 94 in Singapore, was the youngest sister of Loke Wan-tho. Both brother and sister are avid bird watchers, with the former being a great photographer of birds.

Sir Run Run Shaw, an acquaintance I have met once, barely missed that plane disaster, because he changed to an earlier flight to Hong Kong in pursuit of William Holden, who himself was originally also scheduled to join Loke to visit the National Central Museum down south. Had history taken a different turn, the movie industry of Asia in the second half of the last century might have played out quite differently.

Felix and I discussed briefly the November 9, 1949 defection of twelve CNAC and CATC (Central Air Transport Corporation) airplanes from Taiwan to China. Felix was in Hong Kong at the time and played a role in the subsequent court battle to keep the remaining airplanes, seventy-one in total, on the ground.

I knew well two of the pilots, Jack Young and Leonard Lin, who piloted two of the planes, both owned by CATC, to Tianjin on that fateful day. I also knew Barrister Percy Chen, who fought in court for China to take charge of the remaining planes in Hong Kong. His arguments were at first successful, with the Hong Kong court making a ruling that the planes belonged to New China, the PRC.

Later, the decision was reversed during an appeal to a higher court in Britain, with the planes finally ceded to the USA through a cobbled-together ownership and fire sale payment. It ended, to the delight of General Chennault, through the interference and threat of the US government intervening in the British judicial system, citing behind the scene the higher national and allied interests and priorities during the Cold War. Utimately the planes were shipped to the U.S. in 1952.

Our interview was coming to a close in the last of two mornings that I spent with Felix at his home in New Berlin, a suburb of Milwaukee in Wisconsin. Felix struggled to stand up from his rocking chair. This chair, which he seemed to have been affixed to for both long mornings, had a book stuck on the floor to stop it from rocking.

I offered to give him a lift under his arm, as his legs were weak and a bit unstable. He shook me off and insisted in getting up on his own, staggering a bit to hold on to the four-legged walker on wheels. He was eager to get to his desk. Fiddling with two drawers, he found the winged medal with a twelve-point star given to him as an honor by Taiwan's Nationalist government. From boxes next to the window, he flipped through old black and white pictures to show me images and memories from his past.

As I was rising to leave, I told Felix that, this weekend, I would be attending the nearby Oshkosh Air Show, a once-a-year event when over ten thousand experimental and small planes would be flying in. Also being flown in would be many rare WWI and WWII warbirds. Felix offered a parting comment. Barely standing, with his back bent, and holding on to his four-legged walker, he said with a grin, "Give me a C-46, I can still fly it. It is easy."

At 100 years of age, Felix Smith's spirit is still taking flight.

Felix Smith in younger days / 年輕時的 Felix   Felix's pilot friend Harry Cockrell / Felix 的飛行員朋友 Harry Cockrell

參
與
過
五
場
戰
役
的
百
歲
飛
行
員

從傳教飛行員到雇傭兵飛行員

（本文黑白照片均獲菲利克斯‧史密斯授權同意）

他的手指又細又長，又瘦弱。Felix Smith 緊握著筆，動作緩慢，卻堅定地要在他給我的書上簽名。「致效文，感謝（*withanks*）你為中國航空公司和民航空運的歷史所做的一切—— *Felix*。」這行文字就寫在《中國飛行員——為蔣與陳納德而飛》（*China Pilot, flying for Chiang and Chennault*）這本書的扉頁，我第一次看到有人把「*with thanks*」縮短成一個字。而 *Felix* 的人生可沒有抄捷徑，他的人生漫長又精采。

這本書再版後名字改成了《中國飛行員——冷戰時期為陳納德而飛》（*China Pilot, Flying for Chennault during the Cold War*）。蔣介石的名字被拿掉是因為他在亞洲和全世界的影響力式微。很多親身經歷戰爭的飛行員都曾出書，然而這本書不單單只是其中的一本而已。*Felix* 說，負責再版這本書的史密森尼學會學術出版社，將它選入十本寫得最好的戰爭時期飛行史書。

簽書的這雙手也曾經在袖珍型的平臺鋼琴琴鍵上舞動著，如今，鋼琴蓋著兩塊布，閒置在客廳。*Felix* 在密爾瓦基長大，身為音樂老師的父親對小時候的 *Felix* 有一定的影響，*Felix* 學過鋼琴和小提琴。

就在鋼琴附近的窗邊，成箱的報紙、文件和舊照片堆在床邊，那個空間成了 Felix 的臥房。年初他剛過百歲，年紀大了，身體虛弱，讓他行動不是很方便，Felix 只好把床從二樓搬到一樓，放在客廳的角落。

也是這雙手，曾經緊握著駕駛艙裡的方向盤，在亞洲的五場戰役中，帶著 Felix 駕馭著各種飛機，穿過夜空，飛過暴風和槍林彈雨。「光是一架飛機我就飛超過三萬英里。」Felix 跟我說道。

Felix 年輕時就加入了中國航空公司，在一九四五年二戰末期飛越駝峰。戰後，他在 CAT 公司服務了好長一段時間，這是由飛虎隊傳奇人物陳納德將軍所創立的民航空運公司。事實上，當時的民航空運公司和民間並沒有什麼關係，反而比較像是軍事後勤的空運航空。

從一九四五年到一九四九年的國共內戰期間，整個大陸陷入戰火時，Felix 跟著民航空運公司替國民政府空運部隊和彈藥。當國民黨撤退來台後，戰爭還持續著。後來在中華人民共和國建立初期，Felix 和其他民航空運的飛行員還繼續執行飛往中國的危險秘密任務。民航空運在冷戰期間多場激烈的戰役中，雖然表面上是民航公司但是實際上卻是替美國中情局服務，帶著官方的任務進入東南亞，同樣性質的航空公司還有 Air America 和 Air Asia。

Felix 在加入中國航空和民航空運公司之間，還成為全世界第一家基督教傳教航空公司的機師，飛機由戰後閒置的 C-47 改裝成貨機，負責救災和運送醫療物資。飛機以第一位基督教傳教士聖保羅為名，機身還印了一個被橘色火焰圍繞的紅色愛心，下方的粗體字寫著：「路德會世界傳教」。

雇用 Felix 的就是這家很特別的航空公司創辦人 Daniel Nelson 牧師，他也是一名傳教士。除了聖保

Mandarin Jet Chinese stewardess /
翠華號上的中國空中小姐

羅號外，還有聖彼得號，不過聖彼得號是一架沒有引擎的
C-47，「我們拆東牆補西牆。」*Daniel* 向 *Felix* 坦言，說著
他們如何拆下機組零件，好讓另一架飛機能正常運作。幾
個月後，*Daniel* 和家人搭上澳門航空的水上飛機，不幸發
生意外而罹難。據說當時四名暴徒試圖劫走機上運載的黃
金，一陣混亂中，歹徒開槍打中了駕駛艙內的機師，飛機
因此墜海失事。

不久後，韓戰爆發，*Felix* 繼續留在民航空運。他在書中常
把民航空運寫成「該公司」，許多航班搭載的都是軍方人
員或補給物資，這些都是受美軍委託的。法屬印度支那戰
爭爆發後，民航空運開始在東南亞進行秘密飛行任務，也
開始和美國中情局展開長期的合作關係，*Felix* 則把中情局
稱作「該客戶」。

支援印度支那法軍的行動持續了好幾年，有時要出動像
C-119 這種稱作飛行車廂的大型飛機，直搗奠邊府。民航空
運的足跡也曾到過印尼，負責空投物資，支援試圖推翻蘇
卡諾總統的起義行動，因為美國懷疑蘇卡諾是親共的。

最後是五零年代中期到七零年代中的越戰，民航空運再次受美國中情局委託，多數行動都在寮國執行，期間也有較小規模的任務和行動，像是載赫蒙族的戰士試圖去遏止共產黨的勢力在亞洲擴張。這些任務對飛行員來說雖然很小但卻是很重要，和上述五場的戰役一樣危險重重。

有一次，Felix 剛受完訓，模擬飛行到西藏空降由美國中情局培訓的西藏康巴游擊隊，那時達賴喇嘛流亡到印度，游擊隊準備到西藏阻擾解放軍。Felix 在民航空運的同袍 William Welk 一開始就專門負責這些任務。但是，到了一九六零年，Felix 被派去準備駕駛 B-17 轟炸機，準備執行這項在黑夜中從曼谷起飛的長程任務前，美國政府突然終止所有秘密飛行任務，因為一架 U2 偵探機在蘇聯被擊落，機長 Gary Powers 被俘虜。

好幾次 Felix 和我談起他以前執行過的秘密任務時，他都會用手指抵著嘴巴，露出神秘的微笑，然後小聲跟我說：「我什麼都不說，但是我們多多少少都知道彼此在做什麼。」每次只要講到他們替「該客戶」做的事情時，他都會這樣說。偶爾他會說溜嘴，直接講出美國中情局。每一次他發現說溜嘴後，就會用手指抵著嘴。

但是，Felix 不只出勤軍事任務，有一次，他奉國民政府農業部之命，從紐西蘭空運了一大批綿羊到中國大陸，作為戰後替當地居民復育家畜的種羊。民航空運後來在台灣營運，推出了翠華號的民航服務，和軍機貨運並存，多少是為了要掩護這些秘密任務。

「這本書我寫的大多是關於我的飛行員夥伴，而不是我自己。」他再三強調。但是，讀這本書的時候，很難不被一位在冷戰時期如此特立獨行的人物所吸引。現在戰鬥機都自動化了，飛行員在還沒

Loke Wan-tho on birding trip / 觀鳥旅途中的陸運濤
Kai Tak Airport in 1949 / 一九四九年的啟德機場

看到敵人前，就能按下按鈕擊落敵機，在當年可完全不是
這麼一回事。

「我一些同袍都是非常傑出的飛行員，每次看他們飛，我
都會想乾脆辭職算了。」Felix 說著。我問起他關於我們都
認識的朋友 Harry Cockrell 的父親，「喔！小 Harry，他一出
生我就認識他，他父親老 Harry 是位非常厲害的飛行員，
彬彬有禮的紳士，總是西裝筆挺。」Felix 回憶著。我問他
另一位我們共同的友人陳文寬，今年已經 105 歲了。講到
文寬 Felix 滿是讚美，說文寬在那些最厲害的飛行員中是他
很欽佩的一位。「我從文寬身上學習到許多關於中國人的
事」，他又說。

一九五零到六零年代，民航空運設在台北，「當時，我請
了一個中國廚師，我告訴他『可別煮出 lap sap！』，意思
是垃圾」Felix 說。「但是從廚房飄來的香味，我就知道是
一桌美味的中國菜，但是那不是為我煮的，而是煮給他的
朋友。」Felix 微笑著回憶。

他這本書也寫到了幾個重大空難，其中一起是一九五四年
在海南島附近墜毀的一架國泰航空，飛機遭到兩架中國戰

鬥機擊落。*Len Parish* 是其中一名乘客，他也是中國航空的飛行員，他的家人也在飛機上。*Len* 和兩個兒子不幸罹難，不過，他的太太 *Fran* 和女兒 *Valerie* 都被救生艇救了起來。

我和 *Valerie* 認識多年，因為每年在舊金山的中國航空聚會都會見面。雖然當年媒體大篇幅報導這場空難，卻很少人知道中國政府最後有公開道歉、認錯並且賠償。*Felix* 覺得戰鬥機一定是把國泰（*Cathay*）誤認為美方資助的 *CAT*。

Felix 也向我透漏另一起民航空運的 *C-46* 民航機在台灣附近不明失事，時間是一九六四年，那年亞洲電影節剛好在台灣舉辦。飛機準備從台灣南部起飛到澎湖馬公暫停，這座外島有很多軍事設施，離大陸不到一百英里。機長林宏基有十四年的飛行經驗，相當資深。林宏基畢業於中國空軍官校，是空軍司令「老虎將軍」（王叔銘）的女婿。

在馬公登機的是幾位美軍顧問和兩位中國人，其中一位是駐馬公造船廠的海軍中尉，也是雷達專家，另一位是退休後從商的海軍軍官。他們都沒有攜帶行李，海軍中尉正值三天的休假中，他們隨身帶著兩本機密的雷達手冊，班機繼續飛往台中去接一行名人，以及他們的隨行人員。

由於罹難者中有美軍顧問，因此美國空軍的航空專家被派到失事地點勘查，只是得出來的結果和台灣政府的失事報告大不相同，勘查結果令人非常震驚，他推測，班機是遭到劫機，被迫轉往中國，飛行軌跡顯示飛機在空中來回盤旋，最後墜毀在稻田裡。

簡單地說，這個複雜的間諜故事，經過航空專家的判定，飛行員頭部中槍。而那兩本機密的雷達手冊躲過了機場的查驗，裡面被挖空，形狀剛好足以藏兩把 0.45 手槍。然而，因為時機敏感，兩岸情勢非常不穩定，國民政府不想因為劫機事件造成恐慌，基於安全的考量，這份報告一直沒有被公佈。最後，民航空運扛下了所有責任，以飛機維修有瑕疵為由掩蓋真相。

罹難者中還包括亞洲電影大亨陸運濤。我如果可以早一點發現這些民航空運的空難軼事，就能把這些事情告訴一位老朋友。二零一二年，麥客尼斯夫人（*Lady McNeice*）以九十四歲的高齡在新加坡辭世，她是陸運濤最小的妹妹，兩兄妹都非常熱愛賞鳥，陸運濤更是傑出的鳥類攝影師。

曾和我有過一面之緣的邵逸夫也差點搭上那班出事的班機，他因為要跟威廉·霍頓（*William Holden*）見面，因此提前飛回香港，他原本計畫要跟陸運濤一起到南部的國立中央博物館（*National Central Museum*）參觀。假如歷史改寫，上個世紀後半段的亞洲電影產業發展可能會很不同。

Felix 也和我簡短地聊到關於一九四九年十一月九日，十二架中國航空公司和中央航空公司（CATC）的飛機投誠中國的事件。*Felix* 當時人在香港，他後來參與在法庭訴訟飛機產權的事，訴訟的目的是為了保住剩餘的七十一架飛機。

Jack Young（楊積）和 *Leonard Lin*（林雨水）是其中兩位我熟識的飛行員，在歷史上的那一天，他們各自開著一架中央航空的飛機到天津。陳丕士律師我也認識，他為中國辯

Planes loaded for the U.S. / 載滿飛機準備前往美國

護，爭取讓中國接管在香港的飛機。他一開始的辯護很成功，香港法院判決那些飛機應該歸屬於新中國，也就是中華人民共和國所有。

後來整起案件上訴到英國高等法院，原判遭撤銷，法院將飛機判給了美國，透過所有權和賤賣的方式轉讓。這一切都是因為美國從中介入英國司法，在背後強調冷戰時國家和盟友利益優先的重要性，最終的判決讓陳納德將軍非常滿意。而那批飛機則在一九五二年運到了美國。

Felix 住在新柏林，威斯康辛州密爾瓦基市的郊區，在他家最後的兩個早晨，我們的訪談即將結束。*Felix* 費了很大的力氣才從搖椅上站了起來，這兩天早上 *Felix* 幾乎都坐在這張搖椅上，為了不讓椅子擺動，下面還墊了書。

他因為腳沒力氣，站的不穩，於是我過去想要攙扶他，但是他把我推開，堅持要自己站起來，蹣跚幾步後抓住了四輪助步器，走到書桌前。他翻了兩個抽屜，找到一個有翅膀裝飾的十二點星星勳章，這是台灣國民政府頒給他的榮譽。他再從窗邊的箱子裡翻出了老舊的黑白照片，和我分享他過往的回憶。

正當我站起來準備離開的時候，我跟 *Felix* 說，這禮拜我會去看一年一度的 *Oshkosh* 航空展，會有超過一萬架飛機參展，有小型機，也有實驗機，還有許多一戰和二戰的戰鬥機。臨別時，*Felix* 撐著助步器駝著背勉強站著，笑著說：「給我一台 *C-46*，我還能駕馭它，這對我來說太容易了。」

即便已經百歲高齡，*Felix* 的鬥志仍然高昂。

Pilots & crew arrived China Nov 1949 / 一九四九年 11 月抵達中國的飛行員和機組員

老嬉皮的老地方

OLD HAUNT
OF AN OLD HIPPIE

Milwaukee / Green Bay /
Oshkosh, Wisconsin – July 27, 2018

OLD HAUNT OF AN OLD HIPPIE

It was 1969 that I first went to Wisconsin to attend university. Within the first three months of my arrival in the US, on different weekends, I went with several of my school mates to their homes - in Milwaukee, in Kenosha, a suburb of Milwaukee, and then in Green Bay at a dairy farm. On a recent trip to America, just short of 50 years later, I revisited the area.

Back in the autumn of 1969, it had just been one month since, in July, America was riding high and elated by the Apollo mission, the first landing of man on the moon, that one small step for man and giant leap for mankind, as Neil Armstrong famously said. The countercultural film Easy Rider had been released just a week earlier. The Woodstock Festival, that pantheon that epitomized the hippie generation, had just finished a week ahead of my arrival on campus.

Enrolling into Journalism and Art as a double major, I arrived on the campus of the University of Wisconsin at River Falls in my best suit, but soon embraced the popular culture of the era and began to dress down, way down, to the level of a hippie. It was only later that I realized my art curriculum was also good training for my career as an explorer. The heavy art books I carried each day, back and forth between dorm and class, prepared me for my backpacking years in the field.

My first roommate was Warren Ward, a history graduate student from Kenosha, a small city between Chicago and Milwaukee. I went home with him on a weekend to visit his father who was a judge. It was a nice home, a house, with a double garage and a yard, a far cry from the apartment I was accustomed to in the cramped spaces of Hong Kong. It was with Warren that I began polishing up my English, from that of my Irish Jesuit training to an imitation of a midwestern American accent.

My street language was learned from a fellow student, Joe Angeles. "Sh*t" and the F word became part of my newly acquired vocabulary. With Joe, a Mexican American, I went to stay near downtown Milwaukee. For the

Self-portrait HM /
HM 自拍照

first time, I learned what living in an attic was like. It was during Thanksgiving, and I found out that is a big deal in the USA.

Another good friend, Steve Dorner, was in the wrestling team at school. He stayed at our same dorm and frequently hung around us Asian students, finding us extraordinary. His curiosity quickly turned to our mahjong game. He became addicted and insisted on playing with us anytime, day or night, despite losing at every game. I went home with Steve to Green Bay where his family owned a dairy farm. Learning to get up at 4am in the morning to milk the cows was an experiential and existential exercise.

In subsequent years, I went back many times to visit my university in the western part of Wisconsin State, not far from St Paul-Minneapolis, including twice to receive honors, once for a Distinguished Alumnus Award and later for an Honorary Doctorate. But I did not have many opportunities to revisit Milwaukee and Green Bay in the eastern part of the State.

The chance came in July of this year. Following filming of a centenarian pilot at New Berlin, a suburb of Milwaukee, my small team and I drove to Milwaukee to visit the Harley Davidson Museum. Despite that the company has been building motorcycles for 115 years, the museum is exactly ten years old. Four hundred fifty great specimens of the motorcycles are kept here. There are icons of the 1960s,

HM's beat up '62 VW camper van / HM 的一九六二年老舊福斯露營車

especially those from the Hippie era, when movies like "Easy Rider", with music by the Byrds and Jimi Hendrix, helped define a young generation tuned into sex, drugs, rock and anti-war sentiments; a generation to which I also belonged.

At college, I could hardly afford a Harley, and instead had a pre-owned Puch, an Austrian motorcycle strangely engineered with two pistons but only one spark plug. Still, at the museum the vintage bikes, especially those made for the military during WWII, fascinated me. There is also a replica of Peter Fonda's Easy Rider long-fork low-rider bike with an American flag painted on the gas tank. The original was of course destroyed in the last scene of the movie as Fonda and his bike was blasted by a shot gun off the road into a ball of fire. Many older Harley riders

US Navy Harley / 美國海軍哈雷
Some early Harley's / 早期的哈雷
US Army Harley / 美國陸軍哈雷

may recall that dramatic scene.

While all bikes, old and new, were immaculately restored, there was but one exception. This single bike, totally dilapidated with rust, even with barnacles grown on it, was embalmed in a glass case like a mausoleum. On April 18, 2012, a Canadian beachcomber discovered a trailer box on an island off British Columbia. Inside was this Harley Davidson bike, a 2004 model Night Train. Its license plate revealed it was registered in Japan, later traced back to its owner Ikuo Yokoyama who lived by the ocean in Yamamoto Japan.

When the tsunami hit Japan's northeast coast on March 11, 2011, the trailer with this Harley was taken to sea, together with millions of tons of other debris which moved along the ocean slowly with its current. Kept afloat with its foam insulated walls, the trailer crossed the Pacific in 13 months until it was found in Canada. Yokoyama decided to donate his bike for it to be enshrined in the museum in memorial to the nearly 20,000 who lost their lives in the devastating tsunami.

Easy Rider Peter Fonda's bike / 電影《逍遙騎士》中 Peter Fonda 騎的復刻版機車
Enshrined Harley of the sea / 封存展出的海中哈雷

Despite it being a Monday, over two dozen Harleys were parked outside in the lot. Some had come a long way from out of State to visit this museum, but we came the furthest, all the way from Hong Kong, though without sporting the headbands and tattoo. Before leaving the museum, I rode on a police Harley for my new portfolio shot.

The following day, we stayed in Green Bay at a close friend's farm. I've known Martin since my National Geographic days. In 1984, when I went to China on a long expedition, Martin and his wife house-sat for me at my home in the Angeles National Forest. Later on, he joined us as our remote sensing specialist, using his NASA background to direct us to several of the river sources and becoming a key member of those expeditions. His training at Caltech and work at NASA's Jet Propulsion Laboratory were critical in assisting me in much of my exploration work.

At Martin's farm I had a short but memorable moment driving a tractor, but could not wait for the first practice weekend of the Green Bay Packers, a football team gradually making a come-back from the 1960s heyday of being the champions year after year.

One of the highlights of this trip was the visit to the Marine Museum at nearby Manitowoc, adjacent to Green Bay. This is where, during WWII, 28 submarines were constructed, which served in both the Atlantic and Pacific theaters during the war. One retired specimen, USS Cobia, is kept here for visitors to view. It seems out of place that a shipyard so far inland, beside Lake Michigan, should be building submarines for delivery to and operations in distant oceans.

During my visit, I learned about the difficult conditions of operation inside a submarine in those days. Crammed into canvas bunks with hardly any headroom were over 70 crew members sharing around 50 beds in shifts. Some swing-out canvas bunks were strung above the torpedoes and even in between the torpedoes. The heat at over 90°F could be unbearable, necessitating even the naval officers to wear only shorts with no top, yet even so sweat would flow into a puddle below. While submarine warfare was very effective during WWII, claiming 55% of the total in enemy ships sank, the casualties was also very high. One out of five submariners would not live to return from the War.

I have also learned that a torpedo cost around US$15,000, the equivalent of five houses in those days. Each firing was carefully calculated, as there were only up to twelve torpedoes for each of these submarines, firing from both bow and stern. Another interesting fact was that smoking was allowed, despite the limited space and closeted air. And back in those days, practically all naval officers smoked. On leaving the submarine, I noticed a broom put upside down above the tower. I

HM on Police Harley / 騎上警用哈雷的 HM

Martin preparing breakfast / 正在準備早餐的 Martin
HM driving tractor / 開著拖拉機的 HM

asked why and got the explanation that this was a tradition to signify that the submarine was returning to base, having swept the enemy's ships, sinking all of them in one single battle.

As a finale to my visit to Wisconsin, I stopped at the Oshkosh Air Show. This is also known as the Experimental Aircraft Association Airventure Air Show. I flew in once for this show many years ago and have been eager to return. This year, over 12,000 airplanes of all sorts flew into Oshkosh over the week-long festival of aviation. These included many experimental aircraft and home-made planes. Of particular interest to me, however, were the old War Birds, especially airplanes that flew during WWII. At least twelve DC-3s or C-47s, the later being the cargo version of the former, flew in during that week.

In early years of the gathering in the 1950s, the air show had fewer than 150 visitors with just a handful of airplanes. In 1969, the year I came to Wisconsin, the air show finally moved to Oshkosh and quickly became the largest non-commercial air show in America, and the world. During the week, the control tower here becomes the busiest one in the world. Even the Paris Airport Control Tower paid a visit here to observe how the landing and take-off are done visually and with simple radio commands.

As for me, I need to rush back to Chicago where my flight will soon be taking off for Hong Kong. This visit to Wisconsin brought back many warm memories from almost half a century ago, and I promised myself that I would make time to visit again. Perhaps I will come again in the fall for the foliage, but definitely not during the long and bitter snowy winter, which I barely survived for four years. Not all of my memories are warm ones, but those from the first three months in Wisconsin certainly were.

Martin's old barn house / Martin 家的老農舍

老嬉皮的老地方

一九六九年，為了讀大學，我第一次來到威斯康辛州。來到美國的前三個月，有好幾個週末我都會和同學一起回他們家，也因此我到過密爾瓦基市、基諾沙（密爾瓦基市郊）和綠灣的一個奶牛農場。最近一次回美國，我再度來到這裡，闊別五十年的地方。

時間回到一九六九年八月的秋天，適逢達成阿波羅任務屆滿一個月，舉國歡騰，人類首次登上了月球，阿姆斯壯說出了「這是個人的一小步，卻是人類的大跨步」這句名言。反主流文化的電影《逍遙騎士》在一週前才剛剛上映，而在我到校的一週前，胡士托音樂節這個美國嬉皮年代舉足輕重的盛會，也才剛結束。

我穿上我最好的西裝來到威斯康辛大學河瀑分校報到，開始了新聞和藝術雙主修的大學生涯。但是，我很快地就融入當時的流行文化，穿著開始變得越來越隨興，隨興到變成了嬉皮。我到後來才發現，修藝術課對我成為探險家有很大的幫助。那時，我每天都會背著那些厚重的藝術書本來回在宿舍和教室間，正好對我日後到野外做為背包客有很大的幫助。

我第一個室友是一位歷史系的研究生，叫 Warren Ward，來自芝加哥和密爾瓦基市中間的一座小城市基諾沙。還記得有個周末，我和他一起回家，他的父親是一位法官。他們家真的很棒，有雙車位車庫和一個院子，這和我在狹小的香港習慣的公寓根本是天壤之別。因為 Warren 的關係，我開始琢磨我的英語，從跟愛爾蘭耶穌會的學習，到模仿美國中西部的口音。

我的街頭英語是一個叫 Joe Angeles 的同學教我的，「Sh*t」和 F 開頭的字成了我新增加的用詞。Joe 是墨西哥裔美國人，有一次我和他回到他位在密爾瓦基市區的家，那是我第一次體驗住在閣樓的感覺，當時正好是感恩節，我也才知道原來這一天在美國可是個重要的日子。

另一位好朋友 Steve Dorner，他是學校的摔角隊隊員，和我住同一棟宿舍，因為覺得亞洲學生很特別，所以常常和我們混在一起。他的好奇心很快地轉到了我們的麻將桌。他對麻將上了癮，不管是白天還是夜晚他都要我們跟他打，儘管他每一局都輸。有一次我和 Steve 回到他綠灣的家，他們家從事奶牛農業，早上四點就得起床擠奶，這件每天都要做的工作對我來說卻是個特別的體驗。

往後的幾年，我好幾次回到位在威斯康辛西部、離聖保羅都會區不遠的母校，兩次是為了接受表揚，一次是獲頒傑出校友獎，還有一次是為了接受榮譽博士學位。不過，我卻沒什麼機會回到東部的密爾瓦基和綠灣拜訪。

今年的七月，終於有了這個機會。我和團隊在密爾瓦基郊區的新柏林拍攝完百歲飛行員後，一起驅車來到密爾瓦基參觀哈雷戴維森博物館（Harley Davidson Museum），Harley Davidson 這家公司生產摩托車已經有 115 年的歷史，但是，這座博物館才成立十年。館中保存了四百五十輛亮眼的摩托車，包括一九六零年代，特別是嬉皮年代的經典車種，諸如伯茲合唱團和吉米·亨德里克斯配樂的《逍遙騎士》這類電影，定義了那個年輕世代，一個崇尚性解放、迷幻藥、搖滾樂和反戰思潮的年代，而我，也屬於那一個年代。

念大學時，我根本買不起哈雷機車，但是有一輛二手的奧地利普克（Puch），那輛摩托車的結構很奇特，有兩個活塞，但卻只有一個火星塞。話說回來，這個博物館中的古董機車，特別是二戰年代的軍用車，才是我最感興趣的。館裡甚至還複製了 Peter Fonda 主演的《逍遙騎士》中那輛長柄、壓低車身的摩托車，油箱上還漆了美國國旗。原本那輛早已在電影的最後一幕，跟著 Fonda 騎在路上被散彈槍打中，成了一團火球，很多老一輩的哈雷騎士肯定都還記得那戲劇性的一幕。

這些機車不論新舊，都修復得相當完美，唯獨一輛例外。那輛被放在陵寢似的玻璃櫃中展出，車身佈滿銹蝕殘破不堪外，甚至還長了藤壺。二零一二年四月十八日，一位加拿大的海邊拾荒者在卑詩省外的一座島上，發現了一部拖車，裡面放的就是這輛哈雷機車，二零零四年型號的 Night Train，車牌顯示登記地在日本，最後追蹤到了車主是住在日本山元町海邊的橫山郁夫。

二零一一年三月十一日，日本東北海岸遭到海嘯襲擊時，載著這輛哈雷的拖車和數百萬噸的殘骸，一起被帶到了海中，緩慢地隨著洋流載浮載沉。拖車因為有泡棉隔層，在太平洋漂流了十三個月，最後擱淺在加拿大。橫山郁夫決定將這輛摩托車捐給哈雷戴維森博物館，以悼念在這場無情海嘯中近兩萬名的罹難者。

雖然是星期一，但館外停車場還是停了二十幾輛哈雷機車。有些人從其他州遠道而來，但我們從香港來，可以算是從最遠的地方來的了，只是我們沒有像他們一樣戴上頭帶和刺青。離開博物館前，我騎上一輛警用哈雷，照了張照片。

隔天，我們暫住在好朋友在綠灣的農場。早年我還在美國《國家地理雜誌》工作時，就認識了 Martin。一九八四年，我到中國進行長時間的探險工作，Martin 和他太太還幫我看守我那間位在洛杉磯國家森林的小木屋。後來，馬丁成了我們的遙感專家，借助他在 NASA 的經驗，好幾次引導我們探得河源，並成為我們探險團隊裡重要的一員。Martin 在加州理工學院受過的訓練，以及在 NASA 噴射推進實驗室的經驗，對我的探險工作有著相當大的幫助。

我在 Martin 的農場體驗駕駛拖拉機，那是個短暫卻難忘的經驗。我相當期待 Green Bay Packers 美式橄欖球隊第一次的周末團練，他們是一支曾在一九六零年代連年奪冠、現在又逐漸重新崛起的橄欖球隊。

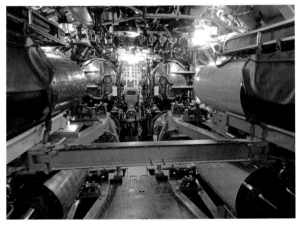

Torpedo with bunks / 魚雷室兼臥室

USS Cobia Lake Michigan / 停靠密西根湖的海鱷號潛艇

這趟旅程中最精彩的部分之一，是到鄰近綠灣的馬尼托沃克附近參觀海事博物館。這個地方曾在二戰期間製造出二十八艘服役於大西洋和太平洋戰場的潛艦，其中一艘已除役的 USS Cobia 就在館中展出。這麼一個深處內陸、位在密西根湖畔的地方，竟曾是負責建造要送往遠洋服役潛艦的造船廠，實在令人意想不到。

參觀時，我才了解當時在潛艦裡的工作環境有多嚴苛，超過七十個船員必須共用五十張帆布床，空間相當狹小，天花板又很低。還有一些床鋪就懸掛在魚雷上方，或甚至魚雷中間。裡面溫度超過華氏 90 度時，讓人難以忍受，逼得連海軍軍官都只好穿著短褲，裸著上半身。即使如此，還是汗如雨下，留下的汗水多到在地上匯聚成小水漥。雖然潛艦在二戰表現出色，被擊沉的敵艦有 55% 就是潛艦所貢獻，但是，傷亡也相當慘重，有五分之一的潛艦船員無法活著回家。

我還得知，一枚魚雷造價約一萬五千美元，在當時可以買五間房子。魚雷可以從潛艇的船首和船尾發射，但是由於每艘潛艇最多只能搭載十二枚魚雷，所以每一發在發射出去前，都要經過謹慎地計算。另一件有趣的事是，潛艦裡雖然空間有限，而且空氣不流通，但是抽菸卻是被允許的，當時幾乎每個海軍軍官都抽煙。離開艦艇時，我注意到司令塔上倒插著一支掃帚，我問了為什麼要這樣擺，原來這是個傳統，象徵潛艦已經擊沉所有的敵船準備返回基地。

在威斯康辛州的最後一站，我來到了奧旭寇旭航空展（Oshkosh Air Show），也有人把這個展稱作實驗飛機航空展（Experimental Aircraft Association Airventure Air Show）。多年前，我曾來過一次，一直想再找機會回來。今年有超過一萬兩千架各式各樣的飛機飛抵奧旭寇旭來參加這個為期一週的航空盛會。其中有很多實驗飛機和自製的機種，然而，我最感興趣的，還是戰爭時代的飛機，尤其是二戰時代的飛機。那周就有至少十二架 DC-3 或 C-47 來到現場，C-47 可以說是貨機版的 DC-3。

在一九五零年代，來看展的人還不到一百五十人，飛機也沒有幾架。到了一九六九年我來到威斯康辛時，展覽地點才移到了奧旭寇旭，而且很快地就成為全美及全球最大的非商業用航空展。展覽期間，這裡的塔台成了全世界最繁忙的地方，甚至連巴黎機場塔台的人員都到場，觀摩飛行員如何只靠著肉眼和簡單的無線電指揮起降。

而我則必須趕回芝加哥，好搭上回香港的班機。這次回到威斯康辛州讓我回想起許多幾乎是半世紀前的美好回憶，我也承諾自己會再找時間回來，或許，等到秋天再回來看落葉吧，但絕不會是冷得要命的冬天，大學那四年的冬天真是難熬。雖然在這裡並非所有的回憶都是溫暖的，但是，剛來到威斯康辛州的頭三個月的確如是。

B-29 Superfortress Bomber / B-29 超級堡壘轟炸機

Flying Tiger P40 Tomahawk / 飛虎隊的 P-40 戰鷹戰鬥機

依揚想亮 出版書目

城 市 輕 文 學

《忘記書》—————————————————劉鋆 等 著

《高原台北青藏盆地：邱醫生的處方箋》—————邱仁輝 著

《4 腳 +2 腿：*Bravo* 與我的 20 條散步路線》————*Gayle Wang* 著

《*Textures Murmuring...* 娜娜的手機照片碎碎唸》——*Natasha Liao* 著

《行書：且行且書且成書》———————————劉鋆 著

《東說西說東西說》—————————————張永霖 著

《上帝旅行社》———————————————法拉 著

《當偶像遇上明星》—————————————劉銘 李淑楨 著

任 性 人

《5.4 的幸運》———————————————孫采華 著

《亞洲不安之旅》——————————————飯田祐子 著

《李繼開第四號詩集：吃土豆的人》———————李繼開 著

《一起住在這裡真好》————————————薛慧瑩 著

《山‧海‧經 黃效文與探險學會》———————劉鋆 著

《文化志向》———————————————黃效文 著

《自然緣份》———————————————黃效文 著

《男子漢 更年期 欲言又止》—————————*Micro Hu* 著

《文化所思》———————————————黃效文 著

《自然所想》———————————————黃效文 著

《畫說寶春姐的雜貨店》———————————徐銘宏 著

國家圖書館出版品預行編目 (CIP) 資料

齊物逍遙 2018 / 黃效文著.
-- 初版 . -- 新北市：依揚想亮人文 , 2018.11
　　面 ;　　公分
ISBN 978-986-93841-9-3（精裝）
1. 遊記　2. 世界地理

719　　　　　　　　　　　　　　　　　107018373

齊物逍遙 2018

作者・黃效文 ｜ 攝影・黃效文 ｜ 發行人・劉鋆 ｜ 責任編輯・王思晴 ｜ 美術編輯・Rene Lo ｜ 翻譯・黃絃瑋 ｜ 法律顧問・達文西個資暨高科技法律事務所 ｜ 出版社・依揚想亮人文事業有限公司 ｜ 經銷商・聯合發行股份有限公司 ｜ 地址・新北市新店區寶橋路 235 巷 6 弄 6 號 2 樓 ｜ 電話・02 2917 8022 ｜ 印刷・禹利電子分色有限公司 ｜ 初版一刷・2018 年 11 月（精裝）｜ ISBN・978-986-93841-9-3 ｜ 定價 1200 元 ｜ 版權所有　翻印必究 ｜ Print in Taiwan